Sing
for Joy

Sing for Joy

ADVENTURES IN WORSHIP FOR CHILDREN

*Developed in cooperation with
the Church Ministries Department of
the General Conference of Seventh-day Adventists*

Review and Herald®
Publishing Association
Hagerstown, MD 21740

This book was edited by Raymond H. Woolsey
The music was edited by Marianne Scriven
The book was designed by Bill Kirstein
Cover illustration by Renée Graef
Interior art by Denny Bond

PRINTED IN U.S.A.

Acknowledgements

The following people worked together in planning this book: Charles L. Brooks and Michael H. Stevenson led out; their fellow workers were Thomas M. Ashlock, Helen C. Craig, Zelma Edwards, Karen M. Flowers, Edith E. Gates, Raquel Haylock, Janice Lenhoff, Noelene Johnsson, Shelton Kilby III, Marvin L. Robertson, Marianne Scriven, Sharon L. Strange, Deborah Wade, and Raymond H. Woolsey.

ISBN 0-8280-0465-X hardcover
ISBN 0-8280-0471-4 wire-o

CONTENTS

Dedicated to our friend Charles L. Brooks, good singer, neat man.

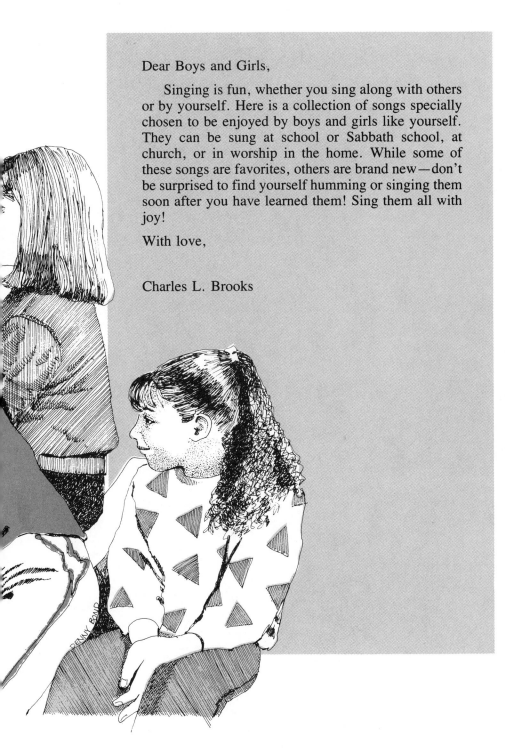

Dear Boys and Girls,

   Singing is fun, whether you sing along with others or by yourself. Here is a collection of songs specially chosen to be enjoyed by boys and girls like yourself. They can be sung at school or Sabbath school, at church, or in worship in the home. While some of these songs are favorites, others are brand new—don't be surprised to find yourself humming or singing them soon after you have learned them! Sing them all with joy!

With love,

Charles L. Brooks

SECTION ONE:

Songs About God

and What He Does for Me

1   Joyful, Joyful, We Adore Thee

Henry van Dyke   *Ludwig von Beethoven*

1. Joy-ful, joy-ful, we a-dore Thee, God of glo-ry, Lord of love;
2. All Thy works with joy sur-round Thee, Earth and heav'n re-flect Thy rays,

Hearts un-fold like flow'rs be-fore Thee, Hail Thee as the sun a-bove.
Stars and an-gels sing a-round Thee, Cen-ter of un-bro-ken praise;

Melt the clouds of sin and sad-ness, Drive the dark of doubt a-way;
Field and for-est, vale and moun-tain, Bloss-'ming mead-ow, flash-ing sea,

Giv-er of im-mor-tal glad-ness, Fill us with the light of day!
Chant-ing bird and flow-ing foun-tain Call us to re-joice in Thee.

PRAISE TO GOD

Sing Praises to the Lord

2

Nancy Harrison   *Nancy Harrison*

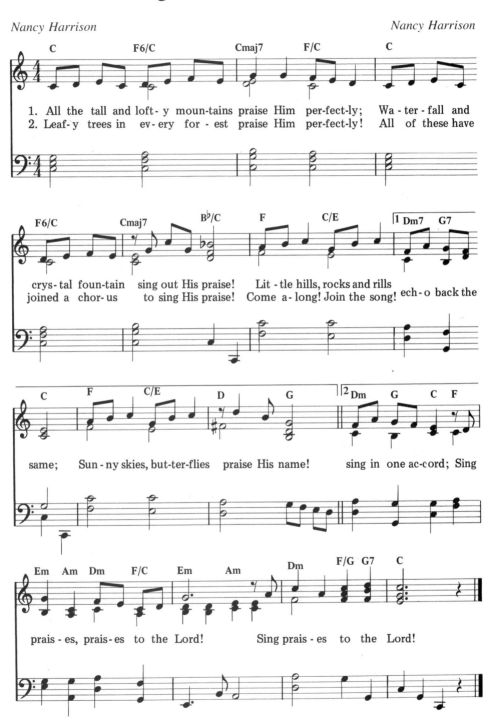

1. All the tall and loft- y moun-tains praise Him per-fect-ly; Wa - ter - fall and
2. Leaf- y trees in ev- ery for - est praise Him per-fect-ly! All of these have

crys- tal foun-tain sing out His praise! Lit - tle hills, rocks and rills
joined a chor- us to sing His praise! Come a- long! Join the song! ech- o back the

same; Sun - ny skies, but-ter-flies praise His name! sing in one ac-cord; Sing

prais - es, prais- es to the Lord! Sing prais - es to the Lord!

PRAISE TO GOD

3 God of Great and God of Small

Natalie Sleeth   *Natalie Sleeth*

1. God of great and God of small,
2. God of land and sky and sea,
4. God of heav'n and God of earth,

God of one and
God of life and
God of death and

God of all,
des - ti - ny,
God of birth,

God of weak and
God of nev - er
God of now and

God of strong,
end - ing pow'r,
days be - fore,

God to whom all things be - long,
Yet be - side me ev - 'ry hour,
God who reigns for - ev - er - more,

Al - le - lu - ia,
Al - le - lu - ia,
Al - le - lu - ia,

Al - le - lu - ia, Prais - ed be Thy Name.
Al - le - lu - ia, Prais - ed be Thy Name.
Al - le - lu - ia, Prais - ed be Thy Name.

1. C

⊕ (to CODA)

PRAISE TO GOD

Name.

poco rall.

3. God of si - lence, God of sound, God in whom the

lost are found, God of day and dark - est night,

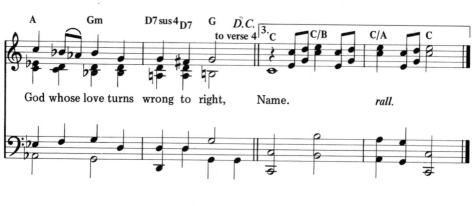

God whose love turns wrong to right, Name. *rall.*

4 Clap Your Hands

Gary Johnson   *Gary Johnson*

Clap your hands, shout for joy, sing to

God ev-ery - one. Clap your hands, shout for

joy, sing to God from sun to sun.

× Optional clap or rhythm instruments.

PRAISE TO GOD

Come and Praise the Lord Our King 5

Traditional Spiritual

CHORUS (Sing Chorus first and after each stanza.)

Come and praise the Lord our King, Hal - le - lu - jah. Come and praise the Lord our King, Hal - le - lu - jah.

1. Christ was born in Bethlehem, Hallelujah,
   Son of God and Son of Man, Hallelujah.
   Chorus

2. Jesus died at Calvary, Hallelujah,
   Rose again triumphantly, Hallelujah.
   Chorus

3. He will be with us today, Hallelujah,
   And forever with us stay, Hallelujah.
   Chorus

4. We will live with Him someday, Hallelujah,
   And forever with Him stay, Hallelujah.
   Chorus

6   Holy, Holy

Jimmy Owens

Jimmy Owens
Arr. by Shelton Kilby III

1. Ho - ly, ho - ly, ho - ly, ho - ly, Holy, ho - ly, Lord
2. Gra - cious Fa - ther, gra - cious Fa - ther We're so blest to b be your chil - dren,
3. Pre - cious Je - sus, pre - cious Je - sus, We're so glad that You've re - deemed us,
4. Ho - ly Spir - it, Ho - ly Spir - it, Come and fill our hearts a - new,

God Al - might - y; And we lift our hearts be - fore You as a
gra - cious Fa - ther; And we lift our hearts be - fore You as a
pre - cious Je - sus; And we lift our hearts be - fore You as a
Ho - ly Spir - it; And we lift our hearts be - fore You as a

tok - en of our love, Ho - ly, ho - ly, ho - ly, ho - ly.
tok - en of our love, Gra - cious Fa - ther, gra - cious Fa - ther.
tok - en of our love, Pre - cious Je - sus, pre - cious Je - sus.
tok - en of our love, Ho - ly Spir - it, Ho - ly Spir - it.

PRAISE TO GOD

Holy, Holy, Holy

Reginald Heber

John B. Dykes

1. Ho - ly, ho - ly, ho - ly! Lord God Al - might - y!
2. Ho - ly, ho - ly, ho - ly! Lord God Al - might - y!

Ear - ly in the morn - ing our song shall rise to Thee;
All Thy works shall praise Thy name in earth and sky and sea;

Ho - ly, ho - ly, ho - ly! mer - ci - ful and might - y!

God in three per - sons, bless - ed Trin - i - ty!

PRAISE TO GOD

Fill Your Hearts With Joy

Timothy Dudley-Smith

Gordon Hartless

Fairly fast, with bounce

1. Fill your hearts with joy and glad-ness, Sing and praise your God and mine! Great the Lord in love and wis-dom, Might and ma-jes-ty di-vine! He who framed the

Words Copyright © 1984 by Hope Publishing Company, Carol Stream, IL 60188. All Rights Reserved. Used by Permission.
Music © 1960 Josef Weinberger Limited. Reproduced by permission of the copyright owners.

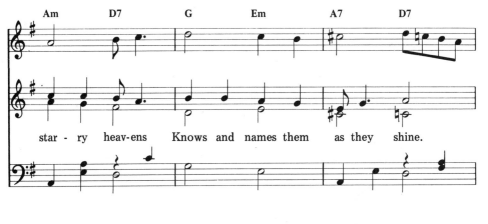

star - ry heav-ens Knows and names them as they shine.

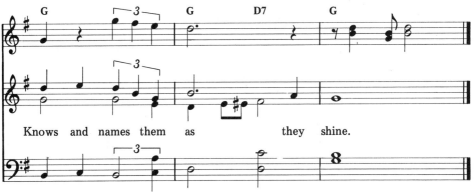

Knows and names them as they shine.

2. Praise the Lord for times and seasons,
   Cloud and sunshine, wind and rain;
   Spring to melt the snows of winter
   Till the waters flow again;
   Grass upon the mountain pastures,
   Golden valleys thick with grain.
   Golden valleys thick with grain.

3. Fill your hearts with joy and gladness,
   Peace and plenty crown your days;
   Love His laws, declare His judgments,
   Walk in all His word and ways,
   He the Lord and we His children;
   Praise the Lord, all people, praise!
   Praise the Lord, all people, praise!

9 Bless His Holy Name

Andraé Crouch

Andraé Crouch

Bless the Lord, O my soul, and all that is with-

in me bless His ho - ly

name. He has done great things,

He has done great things, He has done great

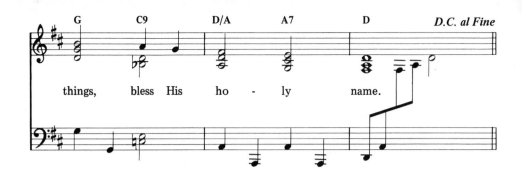

Praise God From Whom All Blessings Flow

10

Thomas Ken   *Louis Bourgeois*

11

Psalm 66

Jane Marshall

Make a joy-ful noise to God,

all the earth; sing the glo-ry of His name, all the earth;

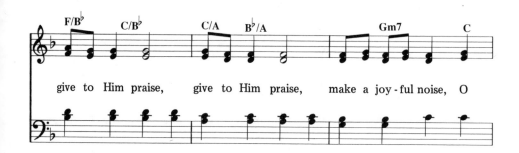

give to Him praise, give to Him praise, make a joy-ful noise, O

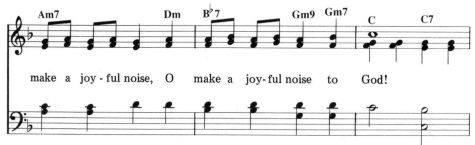

make a joy-ful noise, O make a joy-ful noise to God!

PRAISE TO GOD

12 Praise Him, Praise Him

Arr. by Sharon L. Strange

1. Praise Him, praise Him, all ye lit-tle chil-dren, God is
2. Love Him, love Him, all ye lit-tle chil-dren, God is
3. Serve Him, serve Him, all ye lit-tle chil-dren, God is
4. Crown Him, crown Him, all ye lit-tle chil-dren, God is

love; God is love; Praise Him, praise Him,
love; God is love; Love Him, love Him,
love; God is love; Serve Him, serve Him,
love; God is love; Crown Him, crown Him,

all ye lit-tle chil-dren, God is love, God is love.
all ye lit-tle chil-dren, God is love, God is love.
all ye lit-tle chil-dren, God is love, God is love.
all ye lit-tle chil-dren, God is love, God is love.

Arr. Copyright © 1989 by Sharon L. Strange.

13 God Is So Good

African Christian
Folk Song

1. God is so good, God is so good,
2. He died for me, He died for me,
3. I love Him so, I love Him so,
4. He's com-ing soon, He's com-ing soon,

God is so good,
He died for me,
I love Him so, He's so good to me.
He's com-ing soon,

Come Into His Presence

14

Arr. by Shelton Kilby III

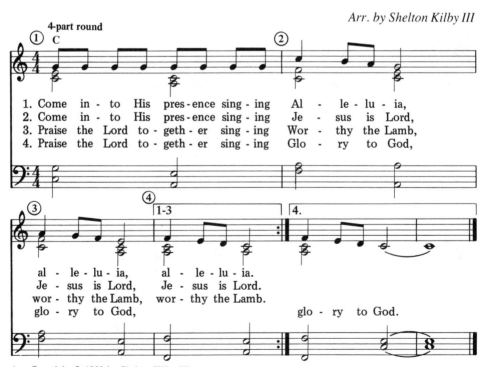

4-part round

1. Come in - to His pres - ence sing - ing Al - le - lu - ia,
2. Come in - to His pres - ence sing - ing Je - sus is Lord,
3. Praise the Lord to - geth - er sing - ing Wor - thy the Lamb,
4. Praise the Lord to - geth - er sing - ing Glo - ry to God,

al - le - lu - ia, al - le - lu - ia.
Je - sus is Lord, Je - sus is Lord.
wor - thy the Lamb, wor - thy the Lamb.
glo - ry to God, glo - ry to God.

15

Praise Him

Traditional

Praise Him, praise Him, Praise Him in the morn - ing, Praise Him in the noon - time, Praise Him, praise Him, Praise Him when the sun goes down.

2. Trust Him, . . . 3. Serve Him, . . . 4. Praise Him, . . .

Alleluia

Traditional

1. Al - le - lu - ia, al - le - lu - ia, Al - le - lu - ia, al - le - lu - ia,
2. He's my Sav - ior, He's my Sav - ior, He's my Sav - ior, He's my Sav - ior,

Al - le - lu - ia, al - le - lu - ia, Al - le - lu - ia, al - le - lu - ia!
He's my Sav - ior, He's my Sav - ior, He's my Sav - ior, Al - le - lu - ia!

3. He is worthy . . . 4. I will praise Him . . . 5. I will serve Him . . .

Lord, We Praise You

Otis Skillings   *Otis Skillings*

Capo on 1st fret

1. Lord, we praise You. Lord, we praise You.
2. Lord, we love You. Lord, we love You.
3. Al - le - lu - ia! Al - le - lu - ia!

Lord, we praise You. We praise You, Lord.
Lord, we love You. We love You, Lord.
Al - le - lu - ia! We give You praise.

PRAISE TO GOD

18 Make a Joyful Noise Unto the Lord

Jimmy and Carol Owens *Jimmy and Carol Owens*

PRAISE TO GOD

All Praise to Thee 19
(also, The Bible, God, Is Wise and True)

Thomas Ken

Thomas Tallis

1. All praise to Thee, my God, this night, For all the bless-ings of the light! Keep me, O keep me, King of kings, Be-neath Thine own al-might-y wings.

2. Praise God, from whom all bless-ings flow; Praise Him, all crea-tures here be-low; Praise Him a-bove, ye heav-enly host; Praise Fa-ther, Son, and Ho-ly Ghost.

3. The Bible, God, is wise and true; Its laws guide us in all we do
   To serve and love you as we ought, To worship you in deed and thought.

4. It tells of your great love for all; Of men who answered to your call
   To trust in you and do your will Your loving purpose to fulfill.

5. It tells of Jesus Christ who came To show your love, to praise your name
   That we might know that you are good, That all the world's one brotherhood.

Orff instrumentation may be used on successive stanzas: alto metallophone, soprano and bass metallophones, and soprano and alto glockenspiel.
Copyright © Choristers Guild 1976, used by permission.
Verses 3, 4, 5 are from "The Bible, God, Is Wise and True," by Lyn Beckwith, copyright, 1965, from *Sing of Life and Faith*, United Church Press, New York, NY, copyright 1969, used by permission of the publisher.

PRAISE TO GOD

20 Join With Us

Edna Bird

David Cooke

CHORUS

Happily

Join with us to sing God's prais-es For His love and for His care,
For the hap - pi - ness He gives us, Praise Him for the world we share.

VERSE

1. Thank Him for the town and coun-try, Thank Him for the sun and rain,

Words copyright © by Edna Bird. Used by permission.
Music © by David Cooke

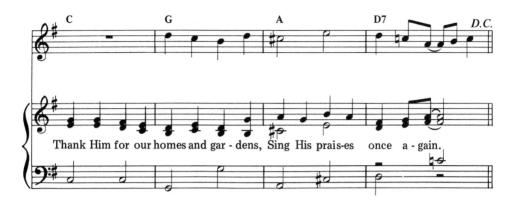

Thank Him for our homes and gar - dens, Sing His prais-es once a - gain.

2. We have eyes to look around us,
   We have strength to work and play,
   We have voices we can use — to
   Sing His praises every day.
   Chorus

3. Praise Him in your words of kindness,
   Praise Him helping those in need,
   Praise Him in your thought for others,
   Sing His praises with each deed.
   Chorus

Father, I Adore You 21

Terrye Coelho

3-part round

1. Fa - ther,
2. Je - sus, I a - dore you, lay my life be -
3. Spir - it,

fore you, how I love you.

All Nations of the Earth

Michael Cockett

Kevin Mayhew

CHORUS

Happily

All the na-tions of the earth, Praise the Lord who brings to birth The

great - est star, the small - est flow'r: Al - le - lu - ia.

Fine

VERSE

1. Let the heav-ens praise the Lord: Al - le - lu - ia.

The descant can be sung on ''oo'' or ''ah.'' The text also can be used as a descant if some note values are modified.
© McCrimmon Publishing Co. Ltd., Great Wakering, Essex, England.

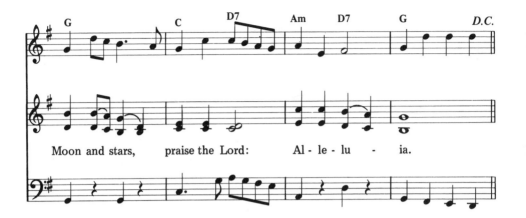

Moon and stars, praise the Lord: Al - le - lu - ia.

2. Snow-capped mountains, praise the Lord:
   Alleluia.
   Moon and stars, praise the Lord:
   Alleluia.
   Chorus

3. Deep sea-water, praise the Lord:
   Alleluia.
   Gentle rain, praise the Lord:
   Alleluia.
   Chorus

4. Roaring lion, praise the Lord:
   Alleluia.
   Singing birds, praise the Lord:
   Alleluia.
   Chorus

5. Kings and princes, praise the Lord:
   Alleluia.
   Young and old, praise the Lord:
   Alleluia.
   Chorus

PRAISE TO GOD

23

Philippians 4:4

John 3:16

Adapted by Dwight Uphaus

Dwight Uphaus

Capo on 3rd fret

For God so loved the world that He gave His on-ly Son,

That who-so-ev-er be-liev-eth in Him should not

per-ish, but have ev-er-last-ing life.

25 His Banner Over Me Is Love

Traditional

Capo on 3rd fret

1. He brought me to His ban-quet-ing ta - ble, His
   lift - ed me up in - to heav - en - ly plac - es, His

ban-ner o - ver me is love, He brought me to His
ban-ner o - ver me is love, He lift - ed me up in - to

ban-quet-ing ta - ble, His ban-ner o - ver me is love. He
heav - en - ly plac - es, His ban-ner o - ver me is love. He

brought me to His ban-quet-ing ta - ble, His ban-ner o - ver me is love,
lift-ed me up in - to heav-en-ly plac - es, His ban-ner o - ver me is love,

GOD'S LOVE

GOD'S LOVE

GOD'S LOVE

For God So Loved the World

F. Tounsend A. B. Smith

26

For God so loved the world, He gave His on-ly Son To die on Cal-vary's tree, From sin to set me free; Some day He's com-ing back, What glo-ry that will be, Won-der-ful His love to me.

GOD'S LOVE

27 Jesus Loves Me

Anna Warner

Wm. B. Bradbury
Arr. by Donald F. Haynes

Bridge to Oh, How He Loves
You and Me, substitute this
measure for preceding one.

GOD'S LOVE

O, How He Loves You and Me 28

Kurt Kaiser   *Kurt Kaiser*

GOD'S LOVE

29 Can You Imagine?

Janette Smart   *Janette Smart*

1. Can you im-ag-ine how it feels to know the God who made the
2. Can you im-ag-ine how it feels to have a Friend who nev-er

earth and sky and sea?   When He cre-at-ed all the
slum-bers, nev-er sleeps?   Can you be-lieve that when He

u-ni-verse, His might-y plan in-clud-ed you and me.
comes in-to your heart and says He'll live there, it's for keeps?

Well, this ex-pe-ri-ence is not im-ag-in-a-tion;

This song lends itself to hand motions. Use your imagination!

GOD'S LOVE

GOD'S LOVE

30 I Am So Glad

P. P. Bliss

P. P. Bliss
Arr. E. M. Stephenson

1. I am so glad that our Fa-ther in heav'n   Tells of His love in the
2. O, if there's on-ly one song I can sing,   When in His beau-ty I

Book He has giv'n. Won-der-ful things in the Bi - ble I   see;
see the great King, This shall my song in e - ter-ni-ty   be:

This   is   the dear-est, that Je - sus loves me.
"O, what a won-der that Je - sus loves me."   I   am   so   glad   that

Refrain G

Je - sus loves me,   Je - sus loves me,   Je - sus loves me;

GOD'S LOVE

I am so glad that Je - sus loves me, Je - sus loves e - ven me.

Alone We Could Not Learn to Read 31

Carol Christopher Drake

From Kentucky Harmony

A - lone we could not learn to read, At school they teach us how;

Nor could we learn to trust un - less Our fam - i - lies taught us how.

We love be - cause God loved us first And lov - ing shows us how.

GOD'S LOVE

32 Wide, Wide as the Ocean

Arr. by Shelton Kilby III

Wide, wide as the o - cean, High as the heav - en a - bove; Deep, deep as the deep - est sea Is my Sav - ior's love. I, though so un - wor - thy, Still am a

GOD'S LOVE

child of His care; For His Word teach - es me

That His love reach - es me ev - ery - where.

I Have Heard Good News Today   33

Native Buzi (Liberian) Tune
From George R. Flora

Abraham Mumol

1. I have heard good news to - day! Who has told you? God's
2. Je - sus is the Son of God! Who has told you? God's
3. Je - sus is the friend of all! Who has told you? God's

mes - sen - ger! Chris - tian, O, Who has told you? God's mes - sen - ger!

This song is most effective when the question is sung by one group and the answer is sung by a soloist or second group.

GOD'S LOVE

34 I See the Love of God in Every River

David Ouchterlony

David Ouchterlony

* F7 for FINAL ending

GOD'S LOVE

GOD'S LOVE

look, I'll find it there. I see the love of God in eyes of old folk

Kind-ly wis-dom shin-ing clear. I see the love of God in lit-tle

ba-bies, Sleep-ing soft-ly, with-out a fear. I see the

GOD'S LOVE

Can You Count the Stars?

35

Wilhelm Hey
Tr. H. W. Dulcken, vs. 1, 3
v. 2, anon.

German Folk Tune

1. Can you count the stars that bright-ly Twin-kle in the mid-night sky?
2. Can you count the wings now flash-ing In the sun-shine's gold-en light?
3. Do you know how man-y chil-dren Rise each morn-ing blithe and gay?

Can you count the clouds, so light - ly O'er the mead - ows float-ing by?
Can you count the fish - es splash-ing In the cool - ing wa - ters bright?
Can you count their jol - ly voic - es, Sing-ing sweet-ly day by day?

God, the Lord, doth mark their num-ber With His eyes that nev - er slum-ber;
God, the Lord, a name hath giv - en, To all crea-tures un - der heav-en;
God hears all the hap - py voic - es, In their mer - ry songs re - joic - es;

He hath made them ev -ery one, He hath made them ev - ery one.
He hath named them ev -ery one, He hath named them ev - ery one.
And He loves them, ev -ery one, And He loves them, ev - ery one.

36

For God So Loved Us

August D. Rische   *Thüringer Melody*

1. For God so loved us, He sent the Sav - ior: For God so loved us, and loves me too.
2. He sent the Sav - ior, the blest Re - deem - er; He sent the Sav - ior to set me free.

REFRAIN

Love so un - end - ing! I'll sing His prais - es, God loves His chil - dren, loves e - ven me.

Jesus Loves Children

Je - sus loves chil - dren wher - ev - er they are, In
Af - ri - ca, Chi - na, Bra - zil, near or far; So
let us each one lend our help - ing hands In
send - ing the Gos - pel to far - a - way lands.

38 More About Jesus

Eliza E. Hewitt

John R. Sweney

More a-bout Je-sus I would know, More of His grace to oth-ers show;

More of His sav-ing full-ness see, More of His love who died for me.

Refrain

More, more a-bout Je-sus, More, more a-bout Je-sus;

More of His sav-ing full-ness see, More of His love who died for me.

Wonderful, Wonderful

39

S. Jones

Arr. by Homer Hammontree

He's Able

Paul E. Paino   Paul E. Paino

He's a - ble, He's a - ble, I know He's a - ble, I

know my Lord is a - ble to car - ry me thru.

He's a - ble, He's a - ble, I know He's a - ble, I

know my Lord is a - ble to car - ry me thru; He

GOD'S CARE

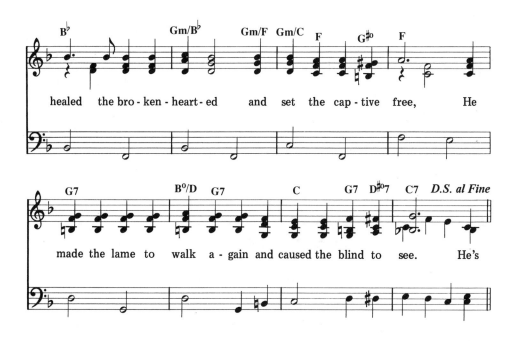

healed the bro-ken-heart-ed and set the cap-tive free, He
made the lame to walk a-gain and caused the blind to see. He's

Jesus Keeps His Promises

41

Don Whitman

Don Whitman

Je-sus keeps His prom-is-es! prom-is-es for me and
you. Je-sus keeps His prom-is-es,

GOD'S CARE

GOD'S CARE

In His Time

Diane Ball   Diane Ball

1. In His time, in His time,
2. In your time, in your time,

He makes all things beau-ti-ful in His time.
you make all things beau-ti-ful in your time.

Lord, please show me ev-ery day, as you're teach-ing me your
Lord, my life to you I bring, may each song I have to

way, that you do just what you say, in your time.
sing be to you a love-ly thing, in your time.

GOD'S CARE

43 He's Everything to Me

Rachel Carmichael

Rachel Carmichael

Capo on 1st fret

1. In the stars His hand-i-work I see, On the
2. I will cel-e-brate na-tiv-i-ty, For it

wind He speaks with maj-es-ty. Though He rul-eth o-ver
has a place in his-to-ry. Sure, He came to set His

land and sea, What is that to me? What is that to
peo-ple free; What is that to

me? Till by faith I met Him face to face,

GOD'S CARE

GOD'S CARE

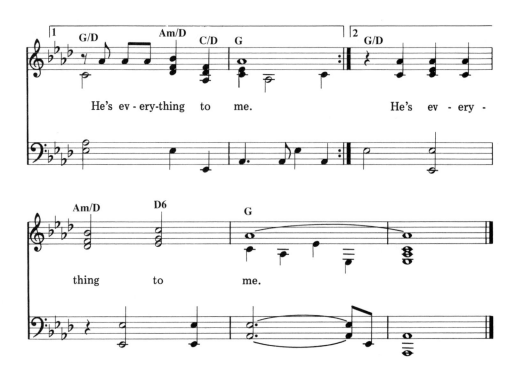

He's ev-ery-thing to me. He's ev-ery-thing to me.

44   Peace, Perfect Peace

Kevin Mayhew   *Kevin Mayhew*

Gently and quietly

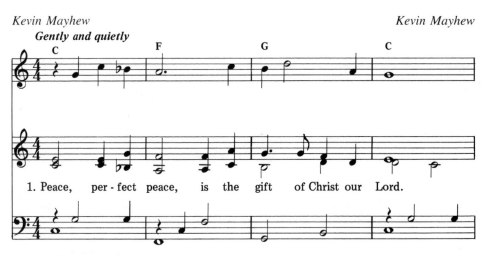

1. Peace, per-fect peace, is the gift of Christ our Lord.

2. Hope, perfect hope, . . .   3. Joy, perfect joy, . . .

Peace, per - fect peace, is the gift of Christ our Lord.

Thus, says the Lord, will the world know my friends,

Peace, per - fect peace, is the gift of Christ our Lord.

GOD'S CARE

45 Anywhere With Jesus

Jessie H. Brown   *Daniel B. Towner*

1. An - y-where with Je - sus I can safe - ly go,
2. An - y-where with Je - sus I am not a - lone;
3. An - y-where with Je - sus I can go to sleep,

An - y-where He leads me in this world be - low;
Oth - er friends may fail me, He is still my own;
When the gloom - y shad - ows round a - bout me creep,

An - y-where with - out Him, dear - est joys would fade;
Though His hand may lead me o - ver drear - y ways,
Know - ing I shall wak - en nev - er - more to roam;

An - y-where with Je - sus I am not a - fraid.
An - y-where with Je - sus is a house of praise.
An - y-where with Je - sus will be home sweet home.

GOD'S CARE

An - y-where! an - y-where! Fear I can - not know;

An - y-where with Je - sus I can safe - ly go.

God Is in This Place

46

God is in this place. His spir-it speaks to you and me. O

come, let us praise His name, rev - 'rent - ly.

GOD'S CARE

47 God Knows Me

John Gowans   *John Larsson*

With a swing

1. There are hun-dreds of spar-rows, thou-sands, mil-lions, They're two a pen-ny, man-y man-y there must be; There are hun-dreds and thou-sands, mil-lions of spar-rows, But God knows ev-ery-one and God knows me.

2. There are hundreds of flowers, thousands, millions,
   And flowers fair the meadows wear for all to see;
   There are hundreds and thousands, millions of flowers,
   But God knows everyone and God knows me.

GOD'S CARE

3. There are hundreds of planets, thousands, millions,
   Way out in space each has a place by God's decree;
   There are hundreds and thousands, millions of planets,
   But God knows everyone and God knows me.

4. There are hundreds of children, thousands, millions,
   And yet their names are written on God's memory,
   There are hundreds and thousands, millions of children,
   But God knows everyone and God knows me.

The Lord Is My Shepherd 48

The accompaniment is optional. When the song is sung as a round, the accompaniment probably should be omitted.

49 All Through the Day

Tom Howard
Tom Howard

All through the day, all through the night,
dwell in His prom-is-es, walk in His light.
Dark - ness shall flee at His com - mand,
All through the day and night we're in His hand.

GOD'S CARE

All Night, All Day

(also, Swing Low, Sweet Chariot)

Spiritual

Capo on 3rd fret

Slowly

All night, all day, An - gels watch-ing o-ver me, my Lord.

*Swing low, sweet char - i - ot, comin' for to car - ry me home!

All night, all day, An - gels watch-ing o-ver me.

Swing low, sweet char - i - ot, comin' for to car - ry me home!

This line may be sung with the other, or separately.

51 All Things Bright and Beautiful

Cecil F. Alexander

English traditional melody
Adapt. by Martin Shaw

1. All things bright and beau-ti-ful, All crea-tures great and small,
All things wise and won-der-ful, The Lord God made them all.

2. Each lit-tle flower that o-pens, Each lit-tle bird that sings;
He made their glow-ing col-ors, He made their ti-ny wings.

3. The pur-ple-head-ed moun-tain, The riv-er run-ning by,
The sun-set, and the morn-ing That bright-ens up the sky,

4. The cold wind in the win-ter, The pleas-ant sum-mer sun,
The ripe fruits in the gar-den, He made them ev-ery one.

5. He gave us eyes to see them, And lips that we might tell
How great is God Al-might-y, Who has made all things well.

This Is a Lovely World

52

Jane Palmer   *Jane Palmer*

1. This is a love - ly world, Birds in the trees a - bove, Sing of a world that's made By a God of love.
2. This is a joy - ful world, Where ev - ery girl and boy Sings of a world that's made By a God of joy.

53   From the Darkness Came Light

Jancis Harvey   *Jancis Harvey*

From the dark - ness came light, From the black-est of nights; Wait for the morn - ing, the sun - light, the dawn - ing; From the dark - ness came light.

Words and music by Jancis Harvey—used by permission.

1. Earth so dark and so cold, what great secrets you hold; The promise of spring, the wonder you bring The beauty of nature unfolds.

2. Jesus was born in a stall, born to bring light to us all.
   He came to love us, a new life to give us;
   Jesus was born in a stall.
   Chorus

3. Jesus died on Calvary, suffered for you and me;
   He rose from the dark and gloom, out of a stony tomb,
   Walked in the world and was free.
   Chorus

4. We have this new life to share, a love to pass on everywhere;
   Time spent in giving, a joy in our living,
   In showing to others we care.
   Chorus

54 Now That Daylight Fills the Sky

Tr. by John M. Neale

Dale Wood

1. Now that the day-light fills the sky,
We lift our hearts to God on high,
That He, in all we do or say, Would
keep us free from harm to-day;

2. "All praise to You, cre-a-tor Lord!
All praise to You, e-ter-nal Word!
All praise to You, O Spir-it wise!" We
sing as day-light fills the skies.

*When sung as a canon, 2nd part enters here.
No. 55 may be sung to this tune.
Copyright © by Lutheran Church Press and Augsburg Publishing House. Used by permission.

CREATION

Every Flower That Grows

Fern Lazicki

1. Every flow'r that grows, Every brook that flows,
   Tell of beauty God has giv'n for me:
   Throughout my life may beauty be
   Deep within a heart from sin set free.

2. Gracious Lord above, Looking down in love,
   Guide my thoughts, my life, in my walk with Thee,
   That day by day the world may see
   Christ, the Lord and Savior, lives in me.

3. All my earthly days, I shall sing and praise
   God the Father, Spirit, and Christ the Son.
   Grant faith when life on earth is done,
   I shall sing with those whose rest is won.

May be sung to the tune of No. 54.

Lord, I Love to Stamp and Shout   56

Ian Fraser

Reginald Barrett-Ayres

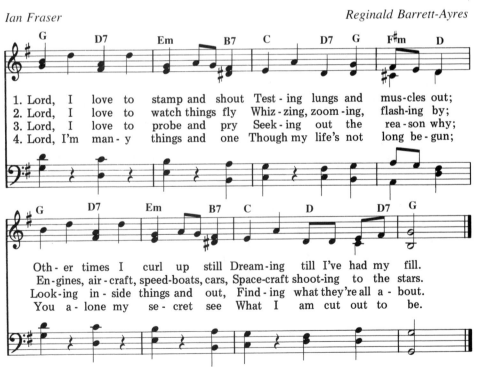

1. Lord, I love to stamp and shout Test-ing lungs and mus-cles out;
2. Lord, I love to watch things fly Whiz-zing, zoom-ing, flash-ing by;
3. Lord, I love to probe and pry Seek-ing out the rea-son why;
4. Lord, I'm man-y things and one Though my life's not long be-gun;

Oth-er times I curl up still Dream-ing till I've had my fill.
En-gines, air-craft, speed-boats, cars, Space-craft shoot-ing to the stars.
Look-ing in-side things and out, Find-ing what they're all a-bout.
You a-lone my se-cret see What I am cut out to be.

The irregular meters are essential to the style of this song. The quarter-note value remains constant.

57 God Made Our Hands

Jill Jackson and Sy Miller

Arr. by Hawley Ades

God made our hands to give and re-ceive His bless - ings, He made each voice for sing - ing a hap - py song, God made our feet to walk on a path of rain - bows,

CREATION

CREATION

Won - der of all, He gave us a gift so spe - cial,

God gave us a heart to share His love.

ff

58 We Grow in Many Different Ways

M. Dosia Carlson

Scottish Psalter

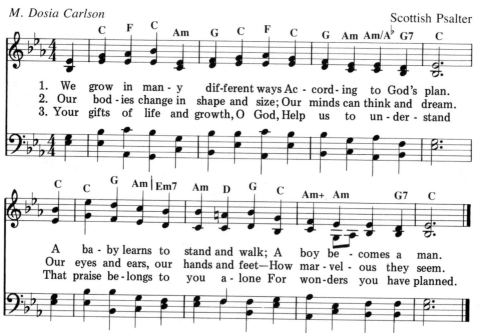

1. We grow in man - y dif-ferent ways Ac - cord-ing to God's plan.
2. Our bod - ies change in shape and size; Our minds can think and dream.
3. Your gifts of life and growth, O God, Help us to un - der - stand

A ba - by learns to stand and walk; A boy be - comes a man.
Our eyes and ears, our hands and feet—How mar - vel - ous they seem.
That praise be - longs to you a - lone For won-ders you have planned.

Words by Dosia Carlson, 555 W. Glendale Ave., Phoenix, AZ 85021, phone (602) 274-5022. Used by permission.

CREATION

We Grow in Many Different Ways 59

M. Dosia Carlson

Perry Beach

1. We grow in man - y dif - ferent ways Ac - cord - ing
2. Our bod - ies change in shape and size; Our minds can
3. Your gifts of life and growth, O God, Help us to

to God's plan. A ba - by learns to
think and dream. Our eyes and ears, our
un - der - stand That praise be - longs to

stand and walk; A boy be - comes a man.
hands and feet— How mar - vel - ous they seem.
you a - lone For won - ders you have planned.

Words by Dosia Carlson, 555 W. Glendale Ave., Phoenix, AZ 85021, phone (602) 274-5022. Used by permission.
Music Copyright © 1985 by Review and Herald® Publishing Association.

CREATION

60

Think of a World
Without Any Flowers

Doreen Newport

Graham Westcott

Smooth and flowing

1. Think of a world with - out an - y flow - ers, Think of a world with -
out an - y trees, Think of a sky with - out an - y sun - shine,
Think of the air with - out an - y breeze. We thank You, Lord, for

CREATION

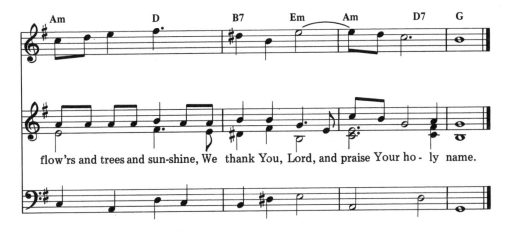

flow'rs and trees and sun-shine, We thank You, Lord, and praise Your ho - ly name.

2. Think of a world without any animals,
   Think of a field without any herd,
   Think of a stream without any fishes,
   Think of a dawn without any bird.
   We thank You, Lord, for all Your living creatures,
   We thank You, Lord, and praise Your holy name.

3. Think of a world without any people,
   Think of a street with no one living there,
   Think of a town without any houses,
   No one to love and nobody to care.
   We thank You, Lord, for families and friendships,
   We thank You, Lord, and praise Your holy name.

CREATION

61 Saints of God

Max V. Exner   *Max V. Exner*

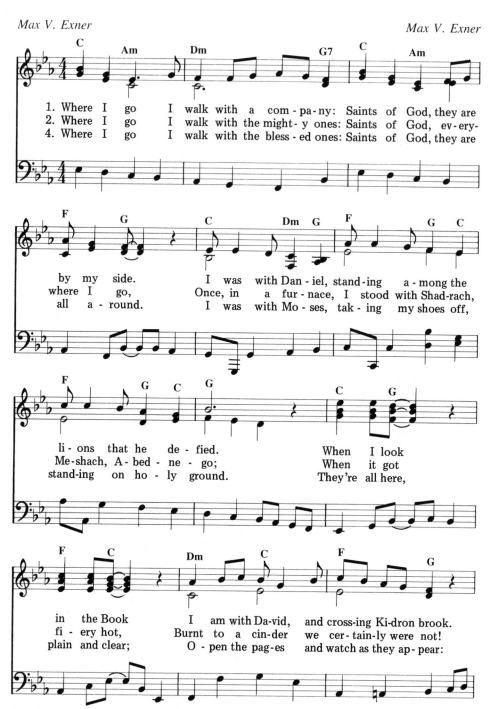

1. Where I go I walk with a com-pa-ny: Saints of God, they are
2. Where I go I walk with the might-y ones: Saints of God, ev-ery-
4. Where I go I walk with the bless-ed ones: Saints of God, they are

by my side. I was with Dan-iel, stand-ing a-mong the
where I go, Once, in a fur-nace, I stood with Shad-rach,
all a-round. I was with Mo-ses, tak-ing my shoes off,

li-ons that he de-fied. When I look
Me-shach, A-bed-ne-go; When it got
stand-ing on ho-ly ground. They're all here,

in the Book I am with Da-vid, and cross-ing Ki-dron brook.
fi-ery hot, Burnt to a cin-der we cer-tain-ly were not!
plain and clear; O-pen the pag-es and watch as they ap-pear:

BIBLE

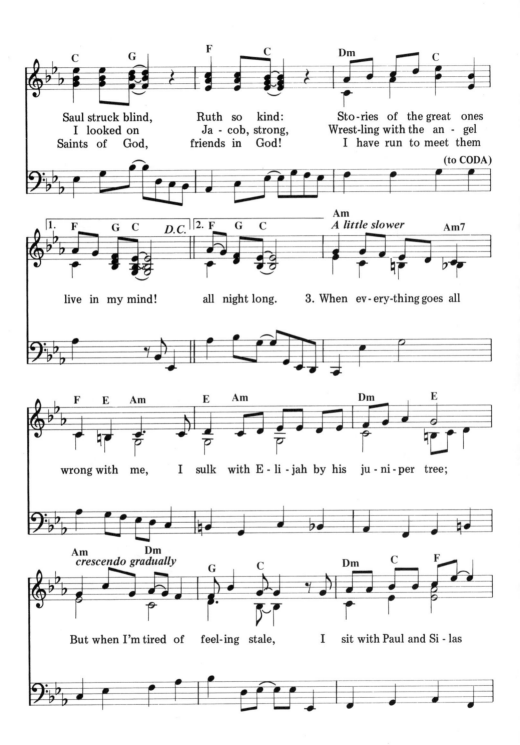

Saul struck blind, Ruth so kind: Sto-ries of the great ones
I looked on Ja - cob, strong, Wrest-ling with the an - gel
Saints of God, friends in God! I have run to meet them

(to CODA)

1. live in my mind! 2. all night long. 3. When ev-ery-thing goes all

A little slower

wrong with me, I sulk with E - li - jah by his ju - ni-per tree;

crescendo gradually

But when I'm tired of feel-ing stale, I sit with Paul and Si - las

BIBLE

sing-ing in jail! where they have trod; I will al-ways walk with

saints of God!

62 The Wise Man and the Foolish Man

Unknown

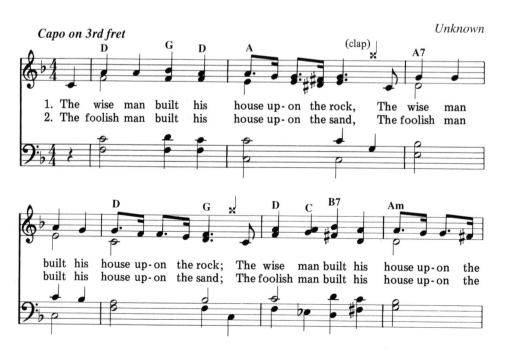

Capo on 3rd fret

1. The wise man built his house up-on the rock, The wise man
2. The foolish man built his house up-on the sand, The foolish man

built his house up-on the rock; The wise man built his house up-on the
built his house up-on the sand; The foolish man built his house up-on the

rock,
sand, And the rains came tum-bling down. The rains came down and the

floods came up; The rains came down and the floods came up, The

rains came down and the floods came up, And the house on the rock stood fast.
And the house on the sand went smash.

𝄎 - *Optional clap or rhythm instruments.*

63 There Were Twelve Disciples

Unknown   George A. Minor

Capo on 3rd fret

There were twelve dis-ci-ples Je-sus called to help Him: Si-mon Pe-ter,

An-drew, James, his broth-er John; Phil-ip, Thom-as, Mat-thew,

James, the son of Al-pheus, Thad-deus, Si-mon, Ju-das, and Bar-thol-o-mew.

CHORUS

He has called us, too; He has called us, too. We are His dis-

64 Deep and Wide

Traditional

Capo on 3rd fret

Deep and wide, deep and wide, There's a
foun-tain flow-ing deep and wide.
Deep and wide, deep and wide, There's a
foun-tain flow-ing deep and wide. wide.

SALVATION

I'm So Happy

Stanton W. Gavitt   *Stanton W. Gavitt*

I'm so hap-py and here's the rea-son why— Je-sus took my

bur-den all a-way; Now I'm sing-ing as the days go by—

Je-sus took my bur-den all a-way. Once my heart was heav-y with a

load of sin, Je-sus took the load and gave me peace with-in. Now I'm

sing-ing as the days go by— Je-sus took my bur-den all a-way.

SALVATION

66 Water of Life

Christian Strover

Christian Strover

Joyfully

1. Have you heard the rain-drops drum-ming on the roof-tops? Have you heard the
rain-drops drip-ping on the ground? Have you heard the rain-drops
splash-ing in the streams and run-ning to the riv-ers all a-round?

CHORUS

There's wa-ter, wa-ter of life, Je-sus gives us the

SALVATION

wa - ter of life; There's wa - ter, wa - ter of life, Je - sus gives us the wa - ter of life.

2. There's a busy workman digging in the desert,
Digging with a spade that flashes in the sun;
Soon there will be water rising in the wellshaft,
spilling from the bucket as it comes.
Chorus

3. Nobody can live who hasn't any water,
When the land is dry then nothing much grows;
Jesus gives us life if we drink the living water,
sing it so that everybody knows.
Chorus

67 Seek Ye First

Karen Lafferty
Capo on 3rd fret

Karen Lafferty

Hal - le - lu - jah.

Seek ye first the king - dom of God

Hal - le - lu - jah.

And His righ - teous - ness;

Hal - le - lu - jah.

And all these things shall be add - ed un - to you.

© 1972 Maranatha! Music.

Hal - le - lu, hal - le - lu - jah.

Hal - le - lu, hal - le - lu - jah.

2. Man shall not live by bread alone
   But by every word
   That proceeds from the mouth of God
   Hallelu, Hallelujah.

3. Ask and it shall be given unto you
   Seek and you shall find
   Knock and it shall be opened unto you.
   Hallelu, Hallelujah.

SALVATION

68 Redeemed!

Fanny J. Crosby

A. L. Butler

Capo on 3rd fret

1. Re-deemed, how I love to pro-claim it! Re-deemed by the blood of the Lamb; Re-deemed thro' His in-fi-nite mer-cy, His child, and for-ev-er, I am.
2. I think of my bless-ed Re-deem-er, I think of Him all the day long; I sing, for I can-not be si-lent; His love is the theme of my song.
3. I know I shall see in His beau-ty The King in whose law I de-light, Who lov-ing-ly guard-eth my foot-steps, And giv-eth me songs in the night.

Refrain *Harmony*

Re-deemed, re-deemed, Re-

SALVATION

69 Amigos de Cristo

John Ylvisaker   *John Ylvisaker*

A - mi - gos de Cris - to; We're friends of the Lord, A -
mi - gos de Cris - to; We're friends of the Lord; For
we've been for - giv - en And we've been re - stored, A -
mi - gos de Cris - to; We're friends of the Lord.

SALVATION

O Come, All Ye Faithful

Tr. by Frederick Oakley

Cantus Diversi

1. O come, all ye faith-ful, joy-ful and tri-um-phant, O come ye, O come ye to Beth - le - hem! Come and be-hold Him born the King of an - gels!
2. Sing, choirs of an - gels, sing in ex-ul-ta - tion, O sing, all ye cit-i-zens of heaven a - bove! Glo-ry to God, all glo-ry in the high - est!
3. Yea, Lord, we greet Thee, born this hap-py morn - ing, Je - sus, to Thee be all glo - ry given; Word of the Fa - ther, now in flesh ap-pear - ing!

Refrain

O come, let us a - dore Him, O come, let us a - dore Him, O come, let us a - dore Him, Christ, the Lord!

71   O Little Town of Bethlehem

Phillips Brooks   L. H. Redner

1. O little town of Bethlehem, How still we see thee lie!
2. O holy Child of Bethlehem, Descend to us, we pray;

A-bove thy deep and dream-less sleep The silent stars go by;
Cast out our sin and enter in— Be born in us today.

Yet in thy dark streets shin-eth The ever-lasting light;
We hear the Christmas an-gels The great glad ti-dings tell—

The hopes and fears of all the years Are met in thee to-night.
Oh, come to us, a-bide with us, Our Lord Im-man-u-el!

BIRTH OF CHRIST

O Little Town of Bethlehem 72

Traditional English Melody
Arr. by Ralph Vaughan Williams

Phillips Brooks

1. O little town of Bethlehem, How still we see thee lie!
2. O holy Child of Bethlehem, Descend to us, we pray;

A - bove thy deep and dreamless sleep The silent stars go by;
Cast out our sin and enter in— Be born in us today.

Yet in thy dark streets shineth The everlasting light;
We hear the Christmas angels The great glad tidings tell—

The hopes and fears of all the years Are met in thee tonight.
Oh, come to us, abide with us, Our Lord Immanuel!

73 Away in a Manger

Unknown
Capo on 3rd fret

1. A-way in a man-ger, no crib for a bed, The
2. The cat-tle are low-ing, the ba-by a-wakes, But
3. Be near me, Lord Je-sus; I ask Thee to stay Close

lit-tle Lord Je-sus laid down His sweet head. The
lit-tle Lord Je-sus no cry-ing He makes. I
by me for-ev-er, and love me, I pray. Bless

stars in the bright sky looked down where He lay, The
love Thee, Lord Je-sus! look down from the sky, And
all the dear chil-dren in Thy ten-der care, And

lit-tle Lord Je-sus a-sleep on the hay.
stay by my side till the morn-ing is nigh.
fit us for heav-en, to live with Thee there.

Alternate tune at No. 74.
Arr. from the *Australian Hymnal* by permission of the Australian Hymn Book Co.

Away in a Manger

Unknown

Arr. by Sharon L. Strange

1. A - way in a man - ger, no crib for a bed,
2. The cat - tle are low - ing, the ba - by a - wakes,
3. Be near me, Lord Je - sus; I ask Thee to stay

The lit - tle Lord Je - sus laid down His sweet head.
But lit - tle Lord Je - sus no cry - ing He makes.
Close by me for - ev - er, and love me, I pray.

The stars in the bright sky looked down where He lay,
I love Thee, Lord Je - sus! look down from the sky,
Bless all the dear chil - dren in Thy ten - der care,

The lit - tle Lord Je - sus a - sleep on the hay.
And stay by my side till the morn - ing is nigh.
And fit us for heav - en, to live with Thee there.

Alternate tune at No. 73.

Arr. Copyright © 1989 by Sharon L. Strange.

BIRTH OF CHRIST

75 Infant Holy, Infant Lowly

Tr. by Edith M. Gellibrand Reed

Polish Melody

1. In-fant ho-ly, in-fant low-ly, For His bed a cat-tle stall;
2. Flocks were sleep-ing, shep-herds keep-ing Vig-il till the morn-ing new;

Ox-en low-ing, lit-tle know-ing Christ the babe is Lord of all;
Saw the glo-ry, heard the sto-ry, Tid-ings of the gos-pel true;

Swifts are wing-ing, an-gels sing-ing, No-els ring-ing, tid-ings bring-ing,
Thus re-joic-ing, free from sor-row, Prais-es voic-ing greet the mor-row,

Christ the babe is Lord of all, Christ the babe is Lord of all.
Christ the babe was born for you, Christ the babe was born for you.

BIRTH OF CHRIST

Silent Night, Holy Night

Joseph Mohr

Franz Gruber

Capo on 3rd fret

1. Si - lent night, ho - ly night, All is calm,
2. Si - lent night, ho - ly night, Son of God,
3. Si - lent night, ho - ly night, Won - drous star,
4. *Stil - le Nacht, Hei - li - ge Nacht! Al - les schlaft,*

all is bright; Round yon vir - gin moth - er and Child!
love's pure light; Ra - diant beams from Thy ho - ly face,
lend thy light; With the an - gels let us sing,
ein - sam wacht Nur das trau - te hoch - hei - li - ge Paar.

Ho - ly In - fant, so ten - der and mild, Sleep in heav - en - ly
With the dawn of re - deem - ing grace, Je - sus, Lord, at Thy
Al - le - lu - ia to our King; Christ the Sav - ior is
Hol - der Kna - be im lo - cki - gen Haar, Schlaf in himm - lisch - er

peace, Sleep in heav - en - ly peace.
birth, Je - sus, Lord, at Thy birth.
born, Christ the Sav - ior is born.
Ruh, Schlaf in himm - lisch - er Ruh!

Vs. 4 is the German text.

BIRTH OF CHRIST

77 Some Children See Him

Wila Hutson   *Alfred Burt*

Capo on 3rd fret

1. Some chil-dren see Him lil-y white, The Ba-by Je-sus born this night. Some chil-dren see Him lil-y white, With tress-es soft and fair. Some chil-dren see Him
2. Some chil-dren see Him al-mond eyed, This Sav-ior whom we kneel be-side, Some chil-dren see Him al-mond eyed, With skin of yel-low hue. Some chil-dren see Him
3. The chil-dren in each dif-f'rent place Will see the Ba-by Je-sus' face Like theirs, but bright with heav'n-ly grace, And filled with ho-ly light. O lay a-side each

BIRTH OF CHRIST

bronzed and brown, The Lord of heav'n to earth come down; Some
dark as they, Sweet Mar - y's Son to whom we pray; Some
earth- ly thing, And with thy heart as of - fer - ing, Come

chil-dren see Him bronzed and brown, With dark and heav - y hair.
chil-dren see Him dark as they, And ah! they love him too!
wor-ship now the In - fant King, 'Tis love that's born to- night!

78 Now Is Born the Divine Christ Child

Traditional French Carol

Now is born the divine Christ child,
Play the musette, play the tuneful oboe,
Now is born the divine Christ child,
Sing we all and rejoice this day.

Il est né, le divin Enfant,
Jouez hautbois, résonnez musettes!
Il est né, le divin Enfant,
Chantons tous son avènement!

French text appears in italics.

BIRTH OF CHRIST

BIRTH OF CHRIST

79 O Children, Come Quickly

Katherine K. Davis

J. A. P. Schulz

Capo on 3rd fret

1. O chil - dren, come quick - ly, O come, one and all! O
2. How dark is the sta - ble, How dark is the night; Yet
3. He lies in the man - ger, He lies in the hay, With
4. *Ihr Kin - der - lein, kom - met, O kom - met doch all, Zur*

come to the cra - dle in Beth - le - hem's stall, And
see how the man - ger is beam - ing with light. O
Jo - seph and Ma - ry be - side him to stay. The
Krip - pe her kom - met in Beth - le - hem's Stall Und

gaze on the won - der, the gift from a - bove Our
gaze on the Babe in the crib where he lies, More
shep - herds are kneel - ing in rev' - rence and prayer, While
seht, was in die - ser hoch - hei - li - gen Nacht Der

Fa - ther in Heav - en hath sent us with love.
fair than the an - gels that dwell in the skies.
songs of the an - gels are fill - ing the air.
Va - ter im Him - mel für Freu - de uns macht.

BIRTH OF CHRIST

Mary Had a Baby

Traditional Spiritual

Moderato
Capo on 3rd fret

1. Ma - ry had a ba - by, O Lord, Ma - ry had a
2. Laid Him in a man - ger, O Lord, Laid Him in a
3. Shep - herds came to see Him, O Lord, Shep - herds came to
4. Named Him King Je - sus, O Lord, Named Him King

ba - by, O my Lord, Ma - ry had a ba - by,
man - ger, O my Lord, Laid Him in a man - ger,
see Him, O my Lord, Shep - herds came to see Him,
Je - sus, O my Lord, Named Him King Je - sus,

O Lord, The peo - ple keep - a - com - in' and the train done gone.

BIRTH OF CHRIST

Joy to the World

Messiah
Arr. by Lowell Mason

Isaac Watts

1. Joy to the world, the Lord is come! Let earth re - ceive her
2. Joy to the earth, the Sav - ior reigns! Let men their songs em -
3. He rules the world with truth and grace, And makes the na - tions

King; Let ev - ery heart pre - pare Him room,
ploy; While fields and floods, rocks, hills, and plains,
prove The glo - ries of His righ - teous - ness,

And heaven and na - ture sing, And heaven and na - ture
Re - peat the sound - ing joy, Re - peat the sound - ing
And won - ders of His love, And won - ders of His

sing, And heaven, and heaven and na - ture sing.
joy, Re - peat, re - peat the sound - ing joy.
love, And won - ders, and won - ders of His love.

BIRTH OF CHRIST

There's a Song in the Air 82

Josiah G. Holland

Karl P. Harrington

1. There's a song in the air! There's a star in the sky!
2. There's a tu - mult of joy O'er the won - der - ful birth,
3. We re - joice in the light, And we ech - o the song

There's a moth - er's deep prayer And a ba - by's low cry!
For the vir - gin's sweet boy Is the Lord of the earth.
That comes down through the night From the heav - en - ly throng.

And the star rains its fire while the beau - ti - ful sing,
Aye! the star rains its fire while the beau - ti - ful sing,
Aye! we shout to the love - ly e - van - gel they bring,

For the man - ger of Beth - le - hem cra - dles a King!
For the man - ger of Beth - le - hem cra - dles a King!
And we greet in His cra - dle our Sav - ior and King!

83 Go, Tell It on the Mountain

American Negro Spiritual

Adapt. by John W. Work

Refrain

Go, tell it on the moun-tain, O-ver the hills and ev-ery-where:

Go, tell it on the moun-tain That Je-sus Christ is born!

1. While shep-herds kept their watch-ing O'er si-lent flocks by night, Be-
2. Down in a low-ly man-ger The hum-ble Christ was born, And

hold through-out the heav-ens There shone a ho-ly light.
brought us God's sal-va-tion That bless-ed Christ-mas morn.

See No. 84 for alternate words.

BIRTH OF CHRIST

Go, Tell It on the Mountain

Refrain (same as No. 83)

1. He possessed no riches, no home to lay his head:
   He saw the need of others and cared for them instead.
   Refrain

2. He reached out and touched them, the blind, the deaf, the lame;
   He spoke and listened gladly to anyone who came.
   Refrain

3. Some turned away in anger, with hatred in the eye;
   They tried him and condemned him, then led him out to die.
   Refrain

4. "Father, now forgive them"—those were the words he said;
   In three more days he was alive and risen from the dead.
   Refrain

5. He still comes to people, his life moves through the lands;
   He uses us for speaking, he touches with our hands.
   Refrain

He's Alive

Tom Fettke   Tom Fettke

3-part round

The Lord is ris-en from the dead. The Lord is ris-en

as He said. He's a-live! He's a-live! He's a-live!

*After voice (3) has completed the 3rd phrase the last time.

RESURRECTION

86 This Is the Day

Natalie Sleeth

Natalie Sleeth

Capo on 3rd fret
With a bounce (♩=80)

mf detached

This is the day that the Lord hath made! Re-joice! Re-joice, and

be ex-ceed-ing glad! This is the day that the Lord hath made! Re-

joice! Re-joice! Hal-le-lu-jah!

1. Christ has con-quered death at last, Left the tomb that held Him fast!
2. Je-sus lives who once was dead! Crown of glo-ry on His head.

RESURRECTION

87 — He Is Lord

Traditional

He is Lord; He is Lord; He is ris-en from the
dead and He is Lord. Ev-ery knee shall bow, ev-ery
tongue con-fess That Je-sus Christ is Lord.

Gleams of the Golden Morning

S. J. Graham *S. J. Graham*

1. The gold-en morn-ing is fast ap-proach-ing; Je-sus soon will come
2. The gos-pel sum-mons will soon be car-ried To the na-tions round;

To take His faith-ful and hap-py chil-dren To their prom-ised home.
The Bride-groom then will cease to tar-ry And the trum-pet sound.

Refrain

O, we see the gleams of the gold-en morn-ing

Pierc-ing through this night of gloom! O, we see the

gleams of the gold-en morn-ing That will burst the tomb.

SECOND COMING

89 Soon and Very Soon

Andraé Crouch   *Andraé Crouch*

Capo on 3rd fret

1. Soon and ver - y soon we are going to see the King!
2. No more cry - ing there, we are going to see the King!
3. No more dy - ing there, we are going to see the King!

Soon and ver - y soon we are
No more cry - ing there, we are
No more dy - ing there, we are

going to see the King!   Soon and ver - y soon
going to see the King!   No more cry - ing there
going to see the King!   No more dy - ing there

we are going to see the King!
we are going to see the King!
we are going to see the King!   Hal - le -

SECOND COMING

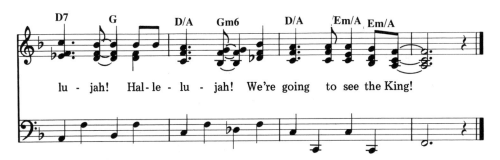

Turn Your Eyes Upon Jesus 90

Helen J. Lemmel
Helen J. Lemmel

SECOND COMING

91   Do, Lord

Arr. by H. Yoss

Capo on 1st fret

1. I've got a home in glo - ry - land that out - shines the sun,
2. I took Je - sus as my Sav - ior, you take Him too,

I've got a home in glo - ry - land that out - shines the sun,
I took Je - sus as my Sav - ior, you take Him too,

I've got a home in glo - ry - land that out - shines the sun,
I took Je - sus as my Sav - ior, you take Him too,

CHORUS

'Way be - yond the blue.
While He's call - ing you.

Do, Lord— O do, Lord— O

SECOND COMING

do re-mem-ber me, Do, Lord-O do, Lord-O do re-mem-ber me,

Do, Lord-O do, Lord-O do re-mem-ber me, 'Way be-yond the blue.

SECOND COMING

92   Jesus Is Coming Again

Jesse E. Strout   *George E. Lee*

1. Lift up the trum-pet, and loud let it ring: Je - sus is
2. Ech - o it, hill - tops; pro - claim it, ye plains: Je - sus is
3. Na - tions are an - gry— by this we do know Je - sus is

com - ing a - gain! Cheer up, ye pil - grims, be
com - ing a - gain! Com - ing in glo - ry, the
com - ing a - gain! Knowl - edge in - creas - es; men

joy - ful and sing; Je - sus is com - ing a - gain!
Lamb that was slain; Je - sus is com - ing a - gain!
run to and fro; Je - sus is com - ing a - gain!

Refrain

Com - ing a-gain, com - ing a-gain, Je - sus is com - ing a - gain!

SECOND COMING

When He Cometh

93

George F. Root
Arr. Sharon L. Strange

W. O. Cushing

1. When He com - eth, when He com - eth To make up His jew - els,
2. He will gath - er, He will gath - er The gems for His king - dom,
3. Lit - tle chil - dren, lit - tle chil - dren Who love their Re - deem - er,

All His jew - els, pre - cious jew - els, His loved and His own.
All the pure ones, all the bright ones, His loved and His own.
Are the jew - els, pre - cious jew - els, His loved and His own.

Refrain

Like the stars of the morn - ing, His bright crown a - dorn - ing,

They shall shine in their beau - ty, Bright gems for His crown.

SECOND COMING

94

Psalm 118:24

Unknown

Capo on 1st fret

This is the day, this is the day that the Lord hath made, that the Lord hath made. We will re-joice, we will re-joice and be glad in it, and be glad in it. This is the day that the Lord hath made.

SABBATH

We will re-joice and be glad in it, This is the day,
this is the day that the Lord hath made.

SABBATH

95 Jesus, We Want to Meet

A. T. Olajide Olude
Tr. by Biodun Adebesin

A. T. Olajide Olude

Je - sus, we want to meet On this thy ho - ly day;

We gath - er round thy throne On this thy ho - ly day.

Thou art our heaven - ly Friend, Hear our prayers as they as - cend;

Look in - to our hearts and minds to-day, On this thy ho - ly day. A - men.

Two drums (of different timbres, if possible) can be used as rhythmic accompaniment.
This song uses a pentatonic scale, F being its tonal center. The notes in the scale are F, G, A, C, D. Any of these notes played during the song will be consonant with the melody. Devise an accompaniment using resonator bells, piano, or any pitched instrument.

Whisper a Prayer

Unknown

Unknown
Arr. by Lyndell Leatherman

96

1. Whis - per a pray'r in the morn - ing,
2. God an - swers pray'r in the morn - ing,
3. Je - sus may come in the morn - ing,

Whis - per a pray'r at noon,
God an - swers pray'r at noon,
Je - sus may come at noon,

Whis - per a pray'r in the eve - ning To
God an - swers pray'r in the eve - ning To
Je - sus may come in the eve - ning So

keep your heart in tune.
keep your heart in tune.
keep your heart in tune.

PRAYER

97 With Folded Hands

Mary B. Blakemore

W. V. Wallace

With fold - ed hands and heads bowed down, Dear Lord, we come to - day; Help us to think of Thee a - lone, And teach us how to pray. A - men.

A Little Talk With Jesus

A lit-tle talk with Je-sus makes it right, all right,

A lit-tle talk with Je-sus makes it right, all right;

In trials of ev-ery kind, Praise God, I'll al-ways find

A lit-tle talk with Je-sus makes it right, all right.

PRAYER

99 The Lord's Prayer

Traditional Caribbean

Rhythmically

1. Our Fa-ther, who art in heav-en Hal-low-ed be Thy name; Thy king-dom come, Thy will be done, Hal-low-ed be Thy name.

2. On the earth as it is in heaven,
   Hallowed be Thy name.
   Give us this day our daily bread,
   Hallowed be Thy name.

3. Forgive us all our trespasses,
   Hallowed be Thy name,
   As we forgive those who trespass against us,
   Hallowed be Thy name;

4. And lead us not into temptation,
   Hallowed be Thy name,
   But deliver us from all that is evil,
   Hallowed be Thy name:

5. For Thine is the kingdom, the power and the g
   Hallowed be Thy name,
   Forever and forever and ever,
   Hallowed be Thy name.

Father, We Thank Thee

100

Rebecca J. Weston

Daniel Batchellor

Reverently Capo on 3rd fret

Fa - ther, we thank Thee for the night And for the pleas - ant morn - ing light, For rest and food and lov - ing care And all that makes the world so fair.

101 Thank You, Jesus

John Hallett   *John Hallett*

1. Thank You, Je - sus, for all You've done, Thank
2. Thank You, Je - sus, for love like Thine, Thank

You, Lord, Thank You, Je - sus, for
You, Lord, Thank You, Je - sus, for

vic - t'ries won, Oh thank You, Lord,
grace di - vine, Oh thank You, Lord,

For Your love and ten - der care, For Your
For Your cross of Cal - va - ry, For Your

PRAYER

G7   **C7**   **F**

Word   and   an - swered prayer,   Thank   You,   Je - sus, for
blood   that cleans - es   me,   Thank   You,   Je - sus, that

G7   **C7**   **F**

all You've done,   Thank   You,   Lord.
You are mine,   Thank   You,   Lord.

Now the Day Is Over   102

Sabine Baring-Gould   *Joseph Barnby*

1. Now the day is o - ver, Night is draw-ing nigh,
2. Fa - ther, give the wea - ry Calm and sweet re - pose;
3. Through the long night watch - es, May Thine an - gels spread

Shad - ows of the eve - ning Steal a - cross the sky.
With Thy ten-derest bless - ing May our eye - lids close.
Their white wings a - bove me, Watch - ing round my bed.

PRAYER

103 Grant Us Your Peace

1. English, *Ottilie Stafford* 3. Spanish, *Espi Wasmer*
2. French, *Marcel Pichot* 4. Latin, *unknown*

Accomp. by Melvin West

3-part round

Capo on 3rd fret

1. Fa - ther, grant us, grant us Your peace; Oh, lov - ing
2. A - coor - de -nous ta paix, ta paix; A - coor -
3. Pa - dre da - nos, tu paz, tu paz; Pa - dre
4. Do - na no - bis pa - cem, pa - cem; Do - na

Fa - ther, grant us Your peace. Grant us, grant us peace;
de - nous ta paix. A - coor - de -nous ta paix;
da - nos, da - nos tu paz. Pa - dre da - nos tu paz;
no - bis pa - cem. Do - na no - bis pa - cem;

Grant us, grant us, grant us Your peace. Grant us,
A - coor - de -nous ta paix. A - coor -
Pa - dre da - nos, da - nos tu paz. Pa - dre
Do - na no - bis pa - cem. Do - na

grant us peace; Lov - ing Fa - ther, grant us Your peace.
de - nous ta paix; A - coor - de -nous ta paix.
da - nos tu paz; Pa - dre da - nos, da - nos tu paz.
no - bis pa - cem; Do - na no - bis pa - cem.

Arrangement Copyright © 1984 by Melvin West.

PRAYER

*One or both of these lines may be repeated for the duration of the canon.

PRAYER

104 God Is With Us

1. Heaven - ly Fa - ther, hear Thy chil - dren, As we come to
2. Keep our hearts and minds from e - vil; Let us walk in

Thee in prayer. Help us al - ways to re - mem - ber
Je - sus' way. Make us lov - ing, kind, and truth - ful;

God is with us ev - ery - where. God is with us!
Keep us safe - ly night and day. Ju - bi - la - te,

God is with us! God is with us ev - ery - where. A - men.
Ju - bi - la - te, Ju - bi - la - te, A - men. A - men.

PRAYER

The Lord Hears Me 105

Phyllis J. Warfel   *Phyllis J. Warfel*

1. The Lord heard Dan-iel and the Lord hears me. The
2. The Lord heard Mos-es and the Lord hears me. The
3. The Lord heard Da-vid and the Lord hears me. The
4. The Lord will an-swer when He hears me. The

Lord heard Dan-iel and the Lord hears me. 'Cause
Lord heard Mos-es and the Lord hears me. From
Lord heard Da-vid and the Lord hears me. The
Lord will an-swer when He hears me. If

Dan - iel prayed to Him, God saved Him from the den. The
char - iots they did flee, Then God rolled back the sea. The
gi - ant he did fight To show God's pow'r and might. The
I just say a prayer, I know that He is there. The

Lord heard Dan - iel and the Lord hears me.
Lord heard Mos - es and the Lord hears me.
Lord heard Da - vid and the Lord hears me.
Lord will an - swer when He hears me.

PRAYER

106 This Is My Prayer

Doug Holck   *Doug Holck*

I want to love You, Lord; I want to serve You, Lord; I want to please You, Lord; This is my prayer. This is my prayer.

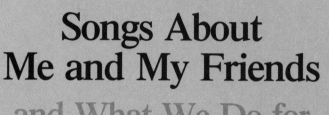

SECTION
TWO:

Songs About
Me and My Friends

and What We Do for
God and Others

107 Smile, Smile, Smile

Carolyn R. Freeman

Carolyn R. Freeman

1. There's some-thing quite pe - cu - liar a - bout this world of ours: Some-times you live in sun-shine bright, some-times you live in show'rs; But if you would keep hap - py when things are look - ing bad, Just lift the cor - ner of your mouth and make be - lieve you're glad, and

2. Some-times you meet with peo - ple who al - ways act so blue; They don't like this, they don't like that, no mat - ter what you do. They nev - er are quite suit - ed with an - y - thing you say, And when you start to do a thing they want a dif-f'rent way, But

CHEERFULNESS

Smile, smile, smile, and keep right on a smil - ing;
it's bet - ter far than

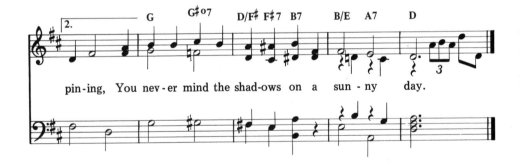

Smile, smile, smile, and clouds will pass a - way.

pin-ing, You nev - er mind the shad-ows on a sun - ny day.

108   I've Got Peace Like a River

Traditional

1. I've got peace like a riv-er, I've got
   (2) love like an o-cean, I've got
   (3) joy like a foun-tain, I've got

peace like a riv-er, I've got peace like a
love like an o-cean, I've got love like an
joy like a foun-tain, I've got joy like an

riv-er in my soul. I've got
o-cean in my soul. I've got
foun-tain in my soul. I've got

peace like a riv-er, I've got peace like a
love like an o-cean, I've got love like an
joy like a foun-tain, I've got joy like a

CHEERFULNESS

riv - er,   I've got peace   like   a   riv - er   in my
o - cean,   I've got love   like   an o - cean   in my
foun - tain, I've got joy   like   a foun - tain in my

soul.   2. I've got   soul.
soul.   3. I've got

CHEERFULNESS

109 I Have the Joy

George W. Cooke

George W. Cooke

Capo on 3rd fret

1. I have the joy, joy, joy, joy, down in my heart,
2. I have the peace that pass-es un-der-stand-ing down in my heart,
3. I have the love of Je - sus, down in my heart,
4. I know the devil doesn't like it, down in my heart,

down in my heart, down in my heart. I have the
down in my heart, down in my heart. I have the
down in my heart, down in my heart. I have the
down in my heart, down in my heart. I know the

joy, joy, joy, joy, down in my heart,
peace that pass- es un - der- stand-ing down in my heart,
love of Je - sus, down in my heart,
devil doesn't like it, down in my heart.

down in my heart to stay.
down in my heart to stay.
down in my heart to stay.
down in my heart to stay. And I'm so

CHEERFULNESS

CHEERFULNESS

110 Teach Me, Lord

Linda Rebuk   *Tom Fettke*

Teach me, Lord; teach me, Lord; Teach me to do Your will. Teach me, Lord; Teach me, Lord; Teach me to trust and o - bey.

I will lis - ten as You speak in Your still, small voice; As You

OBEDIENCE

teach me each day to make the right choice.

Trust in the Lord 111

Trust in the Lord with all your heart, and lean not un-to your

own un-der-stand-ing; Ac-knowl-edge Him in all your ways, and

He shall di-rect your paths, He shall di-rect your paths.

OBEDIENCE

112

Samuel

John M. Nielson

John M. Nielson

Capo on 3rd fret

1. When Sam-uel was just a small boy in the tem-ple, One eve-ning he
2. Then Sam-uel rose quick-ly and ran in to E-li To see what the
3. The boy in the tem-ple had learned a great les-son; He used it when
4. The years have now passed and the Lord is still look-ing; O-be-di-ent

climbed in-to bed; Then he heard a small voice speak-ing
old man might need; But the voice was not E-li's and
he was a man. When-ev-er God spoke, Sam-uel
chil-dren He seeks. And we must be read-y, just

out in the dark-ness, And "Sam-uel" was all that it said.
E-li said frank-ly, "God's voice is the voice you must
said, "I am lis-t'ning; I'll fol-low each step of Your plan."
like lit-tle Sam-uel, To lis-ten each time that He

heed." Say, "Speak, Lord, for Your ser-vant hear-eth;
speaks.

OBEDIENCE

113 Trust and Obey

J. H. Sammis
Capo on 3rd fret

Daniel B. Towner

1. When we walk with the Lord In the light of His word, What a glo-ry He
2. Then in fel-low-ship sweet We will sit at His feet, Or we'll walk by His

sheds on our way! While we do His good will, He a-bides with us still,
side in the way; What He says we will do, Where He sends we will go,

Refrain

And with all who will trust and o-bey.
Nev-er fear, on-ly trust and o-bey. Trust and o-bey, for there's no oth-er

way To be hap-py in Je-sus, but to trust and o-bey.

O, How I Love Jesus

114

Frederick Whitfield

19th century American melody

Refrain

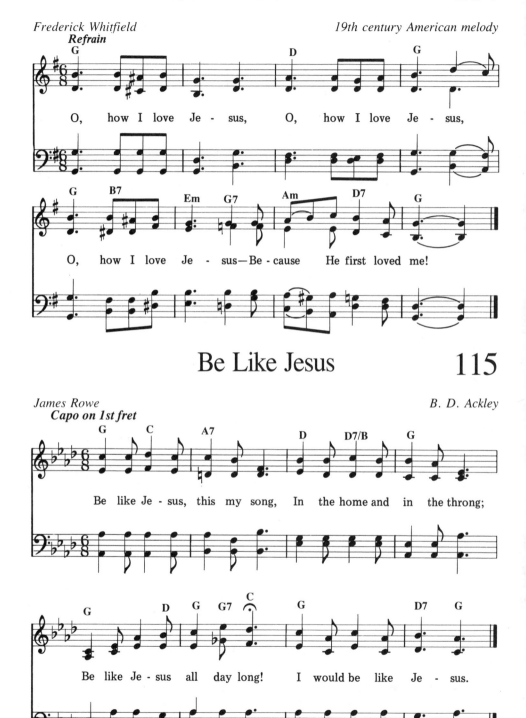

O, how I love Je - sus, O, how I love Je - sus,

O, how I love Je - sus—Be - cause He first loved me!

Be Like Jesus

115

James Rowe

B. D. Ackley

Capo on 1st fret

Be like Je - sus, this my song, In the home and in the throng;

Be like Je - sus all day long! I would be like Je - sus.

116 Dare to Be a Daniel

P. P. Bliss

P. P. Bliss

1. Stand-ing by a pur-pose true, Heed-ing God's com-mand,
2. Hold the gos-pel ban-ner high! On to vic-t'ry grand!

Hon-or them the faith-ful few! All hail to Dan-iel's Band!
Sa-tan and his host de-fy, And shout for Dan-iel's Band!

CHORUS

Dare to be a Dan-iel, Dare to stand a-lone,

Dare to have a pur-pose firm! Dare to make it known!

I Would Be True

Howard A. Walter

Max B. Miller

1. I would be true, for there are those who trust me; I would be
2. I would be friend of all, the foe, the friend-less; I would be

pure, for there are those who care; I would be strong, for
giv-ing, and for-get the gift; I would be hum-ble,

there is much to suf-fer; I would be brave, for there is much to dare.
for I know my weak-ness; I would look up, and laugh, and love, and lift.

118 Give Your Heart to Jesus

Robert Harkness *Robert Harkness*

Capo on 3rd fret

Give your heart to Je - sus, He is call - ing you; Give your
heart to Je - sus, He is call - ing you; Give your heart to
Je - sus, He is call - ing you; Give Him your heart to - day.

I Have Decided to Follow Jesus   119

Traditional

1. I have de - cid - ed to fol - low Je - sus; I have de -
2. The world be - hind me, the Cross be - fore me; The world be -
3. Though none go with me, still I will fol - low; Though none go
4. Will you de - cide now to fol - low Je - sus? Will you de -

cid - ed to fol - low Je - sus; I have de - cid - ed to fol - low
hind me, the Cross be - fore me; The world be - hind me, the Cross be -
with me, still I will fol - low; Though none go with me, still I will
cide now to fol - low Je - sus? Will you de - cide now to fol - low

Je - sus; No turn - ing back, no turn - ing back.
fore me; No turn - ing back, no turn - ing back.
fol - low; No turn - ing back, no turn - ing back.
Je - sus; No turn - ing back, no turn - ing back.

120 We Are Climbing Jesus' Ladder

Adapt. by Geoffrey Marshall-Taylor   *Traditional*

1. We are climb-ing Je-sus' lad-der, lad-der, We are climb-ing Je-sus' lad-der, lad-der, We are climb-ing Je-sus' lad-der, lad-der, Chil-dren of the Lord.

CHORUS

So let's all Rise and shine and give God the glo-ry, glo-ry, Rise and

CONSECRATION

shine and give God the glo - ry, glo - ry, Rise and shine and

give God the glo - ry, glo - ry, Chil - dren of the Lord.

2. We are following where He leads us, leads us,
   We are following where He leads us, leads us,
   We are following where He leads us, leads us,
   Children of the Lord.
   Chorus

3. We are reaching out to others, others,
   We are reaching out to others, others,
   We are reaching out to others, others,
   Children of the Lord.
   Chorus

4. We are one with all who serve Him, serve Him,
   We are one with all who serve Him, serve Him,
   We are one with all who serve Him, serve Him,
   Children of the Lord.
   Chorus

121 Sandy Land

Karen Lafferty   *Karen Lafferty*

Don't build your house on the sand-y land, Don't build it too near the shore. Well, it might look kind of nice, but you'll have to build it twice; Oh, you'll have to build your house once more. more. You bet-ter build your house up-on a rock, Make a

This song lends itself well to hand motions.
© 1981 Maranatha! Music.

good foun - da - tion on a sol - id spot. Oh, the storms may come and go, But the peace of God you will know.

more. Well, it might look kind of nice, but you'll have to build it twice; Oh, you'll have to build your house once more.

CONSECRATION

122 The Journey of Life

Valerie Collison

Valerie Collison

Flowing

1. The jour-ney of life May be ea-sy, may be hard, There'll be dan-ger on the way; With Christ at my side I'll do bat-tle as I ride, 'Gainst the foe that would lead me a-stray. Will you ride, ride,

CONSECRATION

ride With the King of kings, Will you fol-low my lead - er true; Will you

shout Ho-san-na To the low-ly Son of God, Who died for me and you?

123 Right Now

Otis Skillings   *Otis Skillings*

Right now, right now, Com-mit your life right now. De-
cide to live your life for Him right now, right now.

CONSECRATION

I Want to Be

124

Joanne Barrett and Ron E. Long

Joanne Barrett and Ron E. Long

I want to be the ver-y best I can be So I can do what God wants me to do. I want to be the ver-y best I can be So God can do His work through me.

125 Into My Heart

Harry D. Clarke
Arr. by Shelton Kilby III

Harry D. Clarke
Capo on 3rd fret

1. In - to my heart, In - to my heart, Come in - to my
2. Mun - ti mon - ga, mun - ti mon - ga, La - wan - i am -

heart, Lord Je - sus; Come in to - day, Come
bu ye Ye - su; Mu - ka - le mo, La -

in to stay, Come in - to my heart, Lord Je - sus.
wan - i tu, La - wan - i am - bu ye Ye - su.

Vs. 2: Chichewa (Malawi) text.

CONSECRATION

We Are Climbing Jacob's Ladder 126

American Negro Spiritual

Arr. by Melvin West

127 I Want to Be Ready

Harold A. Miller   *Harold A. Miller*

Capo on 1st fret

I want to be read - y when Je - sus comes; I want to be
read - y when Je - sus comes. Earth's plea-sures grow dim While I'm
wait - ing for Him; Lord, keep me till Je - sus comes.

You Must Open the Door

Capo on 1st fret

You must o-pen the door; You must o-pen the door. When Je - sus comes in, He will save you from sin, But you must o - pen the door.

129 We Are His Hands

Jeff Wood

Jeff Wood

1. We are His hands to touch the world a - round us.
2. We are His eyes to see the need in oth - ers.

We are His feet to go where He may
We are His voice to tell of His re -

WITNESSING

WITNESSING

God Calls Us

130

Linda Rebuck

Tom Fettke

1. Be - cause so man - y need to know, It's up to you and me to go. Be-cause so man - y need to know, God calls us, God calls us.
2. Be - cause so man - y need to see, That God a - lone can make them free. Be-cause so man - y need to see, God calls us, God calls us.
3. Be - cause so man - y need to hear, I want to be a vol - un - teer. Be-cause so man - y need to hear, God calls us, God calls us.

WITNESSING

131 Cross Over the Road

Reproduced by permission of Herald Music Service, Farnborough, England.

WITNESSING

Lord His strength to lend, His com-pas - sion has no end, Cross o - ver the road.

2. Would you walk by on the other side,
   When you saw a loved one stray?
   Would you walk by on the other side,
   Or would you watch and pray?
   Chorus

3. Would you walk by on the other side,
   When starving children cried?
   Would you walk by on the other side
   And would you not provide?
   Chorus

132 Give Me Oil in My Lamp

VERSE
Brightly

1. Give me oil in my lamp, keep me burn-ing. Give me oil in my
2. Make me a fish-er of men, keep me seek-ing. Make me a fish-er of

lamp, I pray. Give me oil in my lamp, keep me burn-ing,
men, I pray. Make me a fish-er of men, keep me seek-ing,

CHORUS

Keep me burn-ing till the break of day. Sing ho-san-na,
Seek-ing souls till Je-sus comes a-gain.

WITNESSING

sing ho-san-na, Sing ho-san-na to the King of kings!

Sing ho-san-na, sing ho-san-na, Sing ho-san-na to the King!

3. Give me joy in my heart, keep me singing.
   Give me joy in my heart, I pray.
   Give me joy in my heart, keep me singing,
   Keep me singing till the break of day.
   Chorus

4. Give me love in my heart, keep me serving.
   Give me love in my heart, I pray.
   Give me love in my heart, keep me serving,
   Keep me serving till the break of day.
   Chorus

133   Jesus Bids Us Shine

Susan Warner

Edwin O. Excell

1. Je - sus bids us shine, with a clear, pure light,
2. Je - sus bids us shine, first of all for Him,
3. Je - sus bids us shine as we work for Him,

Like a lit - tle can - dle burn-ing in the night;
Well He sees and knows it if our light is dim;
Bring-ing those that wan - der from the paths of sin;

In this world of dark - ness, we must shine,
He looks down from heav - en, sees us shine,
He will ev - er help us if we shine,

You in your small cor - ner and I in mine.

This Little Light of Mine 134

Arr. by Alma Blackmon
Adapt. from John W. Work

American Negro Spiritual

1. This lit - tle light of mine, I'm going to let it shine, (shine)
2. Ev - ery - where I go, I'm going to let it shine, (shine)
3. All through the night,

This lit - tle light of mine, I'm going to let it shine, (shine)
Ev - ery - where I go,
All through the night,

This lit - tle light of mine, I'm going to let it shine,
Ev - ery - where I go.
All through the night,

Let it shine, let it shine, let it shine.

135 I Will Make You Fishers of Men

Harry D. Clarke *Harry D. Clarke*

Capo on 3rd fret

1. "I will make you fish - ers of men, Fish - ers of men, fish - ers of men, I will make you fish - ers of men If you fol - low Me, If you fol - low Me, if you fol - low Me; I will make you fish - ers of men If you fol - low Me."

2. Hear Christ call - ing, "Come un - to Me, Come un - to Me, come un - to Me"; Hear Christ call - ing, "Come un - to Me, I will give you rest. I will give you rest. I will give you rest." Hear Christ call - ing, "Come un - to Me, I will give you rest."

WITNESSING

SECTION
THREE:

Songs About
Me and My Family

and Our Church and
World Families

136 · A Happy Home

Suzanne H. Clason

Traditional

Capo on 3rd fret

1. God told us how to have a hap-py home,
2. God said, "O - bey your par - ents in the Lord;
3. God said, "Be kind to oth - ers in your home,

Have a hap-py home, have a hap-py home. God told us how to
Do just as they say; mind them ev - ery day." God said, "O - bey your
Oth - ers in your home, oth - ers in your home." God said, "Be kind to

have a hap - py home And live for Him each day.
par - ents and you'll have A long life in My land."
oth - ers in your home And be hap - py ev - ery day."

The numbers below correspond to the numbers in the song. Use rhythm sticks and maracas or other "shakers."
(1) Play rhythm sticks.
(2) Play maracas or other shakers.
(3) Play rhythm sticks and maracas or shakers together.

Love at Home

John H. McNaughton *John H. McNaughton*

1. There is beau-ty all a-round, When there's love at home; There is joy in
2. Kind-ly heav-en smiles a-bove, When there's love at home; All the earth is
3. Je - sus, make me whol-ly Thine, Then there's love at home; May Thy sac-ri -

ev - ery sound, When there's love at home. Peace and plen-ty here a-bide,
fill'd with love, When there's love at home. Sweet-er sings the brook-let by,
fice be mine, Then there's love at home. Safe-ly from all harm I'll rest,

Smil-ing fair on ev-ery side; Time doth soft-ly, sweet-ly glide,
Bright-er beams the az-ure sky; O, there's One who smiles on high
With no sin-ful care dis-tress'd, Thro' Thy ten-der mer-cy blessed,

When there's love at home. Love at home, love at

home; Time doth soft-ly, sweet-ly glide, When there's love at home.

HOME FAMILY

138

God Bless Families

Natalie Sleeth

Natalie Sleeth

1. God bless fam- i - lies ev - ery-where, Thought-ful peo-ple who
2. God bless fam- i - lies great and small, Fa - thers, moth-ers and
3. God bless fam- i - lies far and near, Homes of hap-pi -ness,

tru - ly care, Kind and giv-ing in all they do,
chil - dren all, Dai - ly of-fer-ing thanks a - new,
hearts of cheer, Like the fam - i -ly Je - sus knew,

They let the love shine through!
They let the love shine through!
They let the love shine through!

God bless fam-i - lies old, God bless fam-i - lies new,

HOME FAMILY

Made of peo-ple like me and you!

Descant for one or more stanzas.

HOME FAMILY

139 The Family of God

Gloria Gaither
William J. Gaither   *William J. Gaither*
Strongly
Capo on 3rd fret

I'm so glad I'm a part of the fam - 'ly of God; I've been washed in the foun-tain, cleansed by His blood! Joint heirs with Je - sus as we tra - vel this sod, For I'm part of the

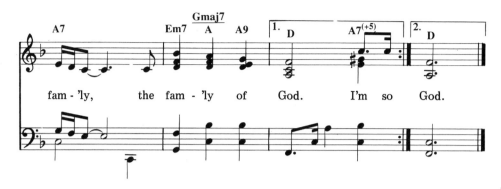

fam - 'ly, the fam - 'ly of God. I'm so God.

Blest Be the Tie That Binds 140

Johann G. Naegeli
Arr. by Lowell Mason

John Fawcett
Capo on 3rd fret 1

1. Blest be the tie that binds Our hearts in
2. Dear Je - sus, be with us to - day, And teach us the

Christ - ian love! The fel - low - ship of
truth and the way. Be with us for - ev - er, and

kin - dred minds Is like to that a - bove.
leave us, no, nev - er, But guide us from day to day.

141 We Are the Church

Richard Avery and Donald Marsh   *Richard Avery and Donald Marsh*

I am the church! You are the church! We are the church to-

geth - er! All who fol-low Je - sus all a-round the world!

Fine

Yes, we're the church to - geth - er.

1. The church is not a
   when the peo - ple
2. We're man - y kinds of
   count if I am

build - ing,   The church is not a stee - ple; The church is not a
gath - er   There's sing - ing and there's pray-ing; There's laugh-ing and there's
peo - ple   With man - y kinds of fac - es, All col - ors and all
nine - ty,   Or nine, or just a ba - by; There's one thing I am

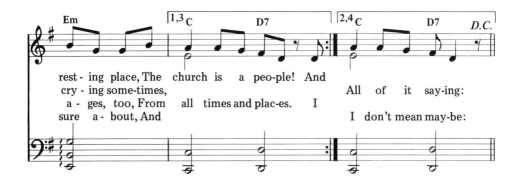

rest - ing place, The church is a peo-ple! And
cry - ing some-times,   All of it say-ing:
a - ges, too, From all times and plac-es.   I
sure a - bout, And   I don't mean may-be:

What Joy It Is to Worship Here 142

Fred Pratt Green

1. What joy it is   to wor - ship here, And find our-selves at home,
2. Yet are no two   of us a - like Of all the hu - man race,

Where God, who us - es ev - ery gift, Has room for all who come!
And we must seek a com - mon ground If we would share His grace.

143 We Are the Church, Everyone

Bonnie Casey   *Bonnie Casey*

Capo on 3rd fret

1. God so loved the world that He
2. God still loves the world His

gave His on - ly true son, To
faith - ful - ness ev - er will be His

tell of His ways and care for His world that's the
peace and His pur - pose, His par - don and power are en -

task that now must be done so
trust - ed to you and to me and

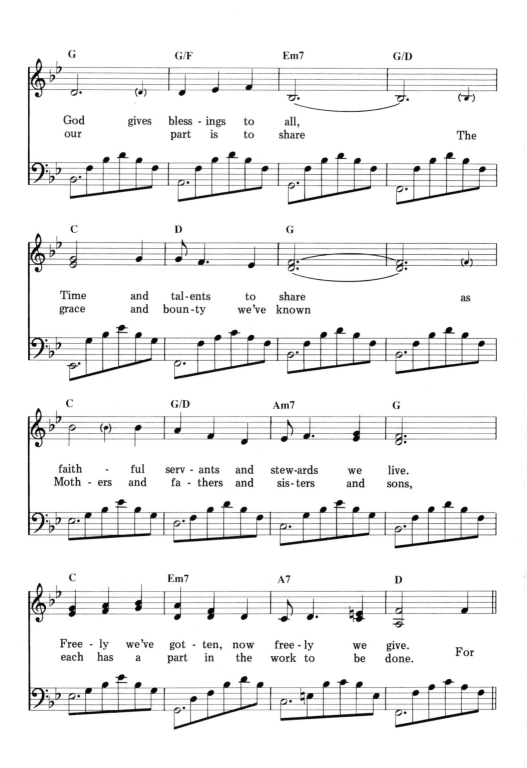

CHURCH FAMILY

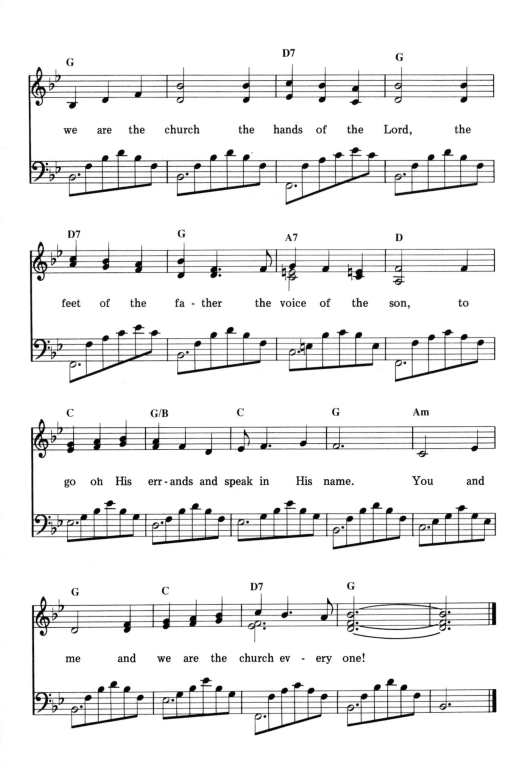

CHURCH FAMILY

I Was Glad

144

I was glad when they said un-to me, "Let us go in-to the house of the Lord."

I'm glad they said, "Let us go in-to the house of the Lord."

Sharon L. Strange

Accompaniment

Ostinato A — Bells, Recorders

Ostinato B — Orff instruments

Ostinato C — Claves, Woodblocks, Rhythm sticks

GOD'S HOUSE

145 This Is God's House

Mary Caldwell   *Mary Caldwell*

This is God's house— His name we would raise.
We come to seek Him, His name we would praise.
This is God's house— with doors open wide. Enter in

GOD'S HOUSE

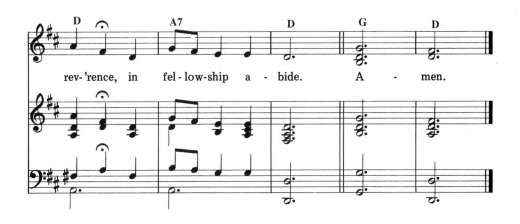

rev-'rence, in fel-low-ship a - bide. A - men.

We Give Our Gifts

146

David Dettoni   *Traditional*

1. We give our gifts, O Lord, What-ev-er they may be, So
2. I give my life to you, To serve you hap-pi - ly, For

peo-ple ev-ery-where may love and serve you joy-ous-ly!
you have giv-en your own Son, A spe-cial gift for me.

147 Father, Accept This Gift

Edith Sanford Tillotson

I. H. Meredith

Fa - ther, ac - cept this gift we bring, Bless it what - e'er it be, Hear Thou our pray'r, Teach us to share All that we have with Thee. A - men.

The Wise May Bring Their Learning 148

Tyrolese Carol
Arr. by Melvin West

Book of Praise for Children

1. The wise may bring their learn - ing, The rich may bring their wealth,
2. We'll bring Him hearts that love Him, We'll bring Him thank - ful praise,
3. We'll bring the lit - tle du - ties We have to do each day;

And some may bring their great - ness, And some their strength and health:
And young souls meek - ly striv - ing To fol - low in His ways:
We'll try our best to please Him At home, at school, at play:

We too would bring our trea - sures To of - fer to the King,
And these shall be the trea - sures We of - fer to the King,
And bet - ter are these trea - sures To of - fer to the King

We have no wealth or learn - ing—What shall we chil - dren bring?
And these are gifts that ev - er The poor - est child may bring.
Than rich - est gifts with - out them: Yet these a child may bring.

Alternate tune at No. 72.

OFFERINGS

149 Shalom

Ancient Hebrew benediction

Sha - lom, good friends, sha - lom, good friends, Sha - lom, sha - lom. Till

we meet a-gain, Till we meet a-gain, Sha - lom, sha - lom.

SCRIPTURE READINGS

Praise to God

Shout for joy to the LORD, all the earth.

Serve the Lord with gladness. Come before him with joyful songs.

Know that the LORD is God. It is he who made us, and we are his; we are his people, the sheep of his pasture.

Enter his gates with thanksgiving and his courts with praise; give thanks to him and praise his name.

For the LORD is good and his love endures forever; his faithfulness continues through all generations.
—Psalm 100.

Trust

"Therefore I tell you, do not worry about your life, what you will eat or drink, or about your body, what you will wear. Is not life more important than food, and the body more important than clothes?

Look at the birds of the air; they do not sow or reap or store away in barns, and yet your heavenly Father feeds them. Are you not much more valuable than they?

Who of you by worrying can add a single hour to his life?

And why do you worry about clothes? See how the lilies of the field grow. They do not labor or spin.

Yet I tell you that not even Solomon in all his splendor was dressed like one of these. But seek first his kingdom and his righteousness, and all these things will be given to you as well.

Therefore do not worry about tomorrow, for tomorrow will worry about itself. Each day has enough trouble of its own."
—From Matthew 6.

Commandments

"The most important commandment," answered Jesus, "is this: 'Hear, O Israel, the Lord our God, the Lord is one.

Love the Lord your God with all your heart and with all your soul and with all your mind and with all your strength.'

The second is this: 'Love your neighbor as yourself.' There is no commandment greater than these."
—From Mark 12.

Other Suggested Readings:

GOD'S LOVE: Matt. 18:10-14; 19:13-15.
THE BEAUTITUDES: Matt. 5:1-12.
MISSION: Matt. 5:14-16.
CHRIST'S RETURN: Acts 1:9-11;
    1 Thess. 4:16, 17.
NEW EARTH: Isa. 65:17, 21, 25.
NEW JERUSALEM: Rev. 21:1-4; 22:1, 2.

TOPICAL INDEX

ADORATION AND PRAISE
All praise to Thee, 19
All the nations of the earth, 22
Alleluia, 16
Bless His holy name, 9
Clap your hands, 4
Come and praise the Lord, 5
Come into His presence, 14
Father, I adore You, 21
Fill your hearts with joy, 8
God is so good, 13
God of great and God of small, 3
Holy, holy, 6
Holy, holy, holy, 7
Join with us, 20
Joyful, joyful, 1
Make a joyful noise, 18
Lord, we praise Thee, 17
Praise God from whom, 10
Praise Him, 15
Praise Him, praise Him, 12
Psalm 66, 11
Sing Praises to the Lord, 2

ANGELS
All night, all day, 50

ASCENSION
(See JESUS: Resurrection)

BENEDICTION
(See CLOSE OF WORSHIP)

BIBLE
All praise to Thee, 19
I am so glad, 30
Saints of God, 61
Seek ye first, 67
The Bible, God, is wise and true, 19
The wise man and the foolish man, 62
There were twelve disciples, 63

BROTHERHOOD
(See LOVE FOR ONE ANOTHER)

CANONS
(See ROUNDS)

CAROLS
(See JESUS CHRIST: Birth)

CHEERFULNESS
I have the joy, 109
I've got peace, 108
Smile, smile, smile, 107

CHOICE
I have decided, 119
You must open the door, 128

CHRISTMAS
(See JESUS CHRIST: Birth)

CHURCH
Blest be the tie, 140
The family of God, 139
We are the church, 141
We are the church, everyone, 143
What joy it is to worship here, 142

CLOSE OF WORSHIP
Be like Jesus, 115
Blest be the tie, 140
Grant us Your peace, 103
Shalom, 149
Thank You, Jesus, 101
Trust in the Lord, 111

COMMITMENT
(See CONSECRATION)

TOPICAL INDEX

TOPICAL INDEX

God made our hands, 57
He's everything to me, 43
Joyful, joyful, 1
Sing praises to the Lord, 2
Think of a world without any flowers,
60
This is a lovely world, 52

GOSPEL
(*See* SALVATION)

GUIDANCE
(*See* GOD: Cares for Us)

HEALTH
(*See* TEMPERANCE)

HOLY SCRIPTURES
(*See* BIBLE)

HOME
(*See* FAMILY AND HOME)

INCARNATION
(*See* JESUS CHRIST: Birth)

JESUS CHRIST
Birth
Away in a manger, 73, 74
Go, tell in on the mountain, 83
Infant holy, infant lowly, 75
Joy to the world, 81
Mary had a baby, 80
Now is born the divine Christ child,
78
O children, come quickly, 79
O, come, all ye faithful, 70
O little town of Bethlehem, 71, 72
Silent night, holy night, 76

Some children see Him, 77
There's a song in the air, 82
Death
Go, tell it on the mountain, 83
God is so good, 13
O, how He loves you and me, 28

Resurrection
He is Lord, 87
He's alive, 85
This is the day 86

Second Coming
Do, Lord, 91
For God so loved the world, 26
Gleams of the golden morning, 88
God is so good, 13
Jesus is coming again, 92
Soon and very soon, 89
Swing low, sweet chariot, see 50
Turn your eyes upon Jesus, 90
When He cometh, 93

Love for Us
Alone we could not learn to read, 31
For God so loved the world, 26
God is so good, 13
His banner over me is love, 25
I am so glad, 30
I'm so glad, 139
Jesus loves children, 37
Jesus loves me, 27
John 3:16, 24
More about Jesus, 38
O, how He loves you and me, 28
Wide, wide as the ocean, 32

Praise
God is so good, 13
Praise Him, praise Him, 12
Wonderful, Wonderful, 39

JUSTIFICATION
(*See* SALVATION)

TOPICAL INDEX

TOPICAL INDEX

Shalom, 149
The Lord is my Shepherd, 48

SABBATH
Jesus, we want to meet, 95
Psalm 118:24, 94

SALVATION
Amigos de Cristo, 69
Deep and wide, 64
I'm so happy, 65
Redeemed! 68
Seek ye first, 67
Water of life, 66

SANCTIFICATION
(See SALVATION)

SECOND ADVENT
(See JESUS CHRIST: Second Coming)

SECURITY
(See GOD: Cares for Us)

SELF-CONCEPT
Lord, I love to stamp and shout, 56
We grow in many different ways, 58, 59

SHARING
(See WITNESSING)

STEWARDSHIP
(See OFFERING)

TEMPERANCE
Dare to be a Daniel, 116

I would be true, 117

THANKSGIVING
Father, we thank Thee, 100
Join with us, 20
Thank You, Jesus, 101

TRINITY
All praise to Thee, 19
Father, I adore You, 21
Holy, holy, 6
Holy, holy, holy, 7
Praise God from whom all blessings flow, 10

TRUST
Teach me, Lord, 110
Trust and obey, 113
Trust in the Lord, 111

VESPERS
(See CLOSE OF WORSHIP)

WITNESSING
Cross over the road, 131
Give me oil in my lamp, 132
God calls us, 130
I will make you fishers of men, 135
Jesus bids us shine, 133
This little light of mine, 134
We are His hands, 129

WORSHIP
(See ADORATION AND PRAISE; CLOSE OF WORSHIP; GOD; JESUS CHRIST: Praise; OPENING OF WORSHIP; TRINITY)

INDEX OF TITLES AND FIRST LINES

INDEX OF TITLES AND FIRST LINES